Speaking Effectively

Achieving Excellence in Presentations

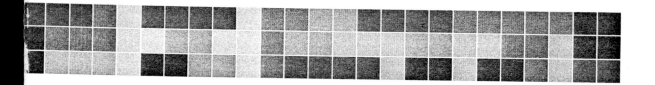

JOHN A. KLINE
Troy State University

NETEFFECT SERIES

PEARSON

Prentice Hall

Upper Saddle River, New Jersey
Columbus, Ohio

Library of Congress Cataloging in Publication Data

Kline, John A.
    Speaking effectively : achieving excellence in presentations / John A. Kline.
        p. cm. - (NetEffect series)
Includes index.
    ISBN 0-13-112833-7
    1. Business presentations. 2. Verbal ability. 3. Public speaking.
    I. Title. II. Series
    HF5718.22.K55 2004
    651.7'3—dc21

                                            2003013517

Vice President and Publisher: Jeffery W. Johnston
Senior Acquisitions Editor: Sande Johnson
Assistant Editor: Cecilia Johnson
Editorial Assistant: Erin Anderson
Production Editor: Holcomb Hathaway
Design Coordinator: Diane C. Lorenzo
Cover Designer: Jeff Vanik
Cover Art: Illustration Works
Production Manager: Pamela D. Bennett
Director of Marketing: Ann Castel Davis
Director of Advertising: Kevin Flanagan
Marketing Manager: Christina Quadhamer

This book was set in Goudy by Carlisle Communications, Ltd. It was printed and bound by R. R. Donnelley & Sons Company. The cover was printed by Phoenix Color Corp.

Pearson Education Ltd.
Pearson Education Singapore Pte. Ltd.
Pearson Education Canada, Ltd.
Pearson Education—Japan

Pearson Education Australia Pty. Limited
Pearson Education North Asia Ltd.
Pearson Educación de Mexico, S.A. de C.V.
Pearson Education Malaysia Pte. Ltd.

11 12 13 14 15

ISBN 0-13-112833-7

Brief Contents

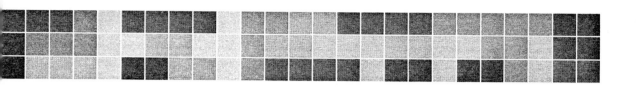

Contents

Preface

This preface is short. For that matter, I've tried to keep the entire book as short as possible yet cover what's really important about preparing and presenting different kinds of talks.

The material in this book comes from three decades of study, research, and teaching thousands of people, from college students to corporate leaders. Even more, this book contains what I have learned during that time speaking more than 100 times a year to all kinds of audiences.

ORGANIZATION

The chapter titles tell the story: (1) Preparing to Speak, (2) Organizing the Presentation, (3) Using Clarification Support, (4) Using Proof Support, (5) Using Humorous Support, (6) Using Visual Support, (7) Beginnings, Endings, and Transitions, (8) Presentation Strategies, and (9) Presentation Skills.

I've emphasized using various kinds of support, because effective supporting material holds listeners' interest and communicates the message. I've also devoted two chapters to presentation—one to strategies, another to skills. Even the best planned, prepared, organized, and supported talk will be ineffective if not presented well.

SPECIAL FEATURES

- *Objectives and Tasks.* Each chapter begins with an objective and tasks or behaviors to demonstrate that readers have achieved the objective.
- *Humor.* Few books on speaking adequately treat the subject, yet it is one of the best tools the speaker has. This book devotes a chapter to the use of humor.

- *Activities.*   Exercises are scattered throughout the book to help the reader acquire and practice skills taught in the book.
- *Supporting Material.*   The book emphasizes the importance of support, so I've tried to use lots of it to illustrate points.
- *Checklists.*   The book has numerous lists on how to adapt to an audience, use various kinds of support material, construct visual aids, and so forth.
- *Writing Style.*   The book is lively and easy to read. I don't use technical jargon. The book is suited for both the beginner and the professional who wants to learn more.

ACKNOWLEDGMENTS

Many people have helped me along the way. My sincere thanks to Sande Johnson, senior acquisitions editor at Prentice Hall, who advised and encouraged me, and to assistant editor Cecilia Johnson, editorial assistant Erin Anderson, and marketing manager Christina Quadhamer, who helped at various stages and who were always so delightful to work with. I also want to thank Gay Pauley, who helped fine-tune the manuscript during copy-editing and production.

Dr. Jack Hawkins, Jr., chancellor of the Troy State University system, and Dr. Ed Roach, executive vice chancellor for Academic Affairs, have been supportive and make Troy State a great university and a wonderful place to work, study, teach, and have fun. A special thanks goes to Dr. Jim Vickrey, professor and chairman of the Department of Speech Communication at Troy State University, Alabama. Not only is he a good friend and a constant source of ideas, but he also provided many helpful suggestions for the final manuscript. This book is better because of his advice. Thanks also to my sister, Helene Mooty, who read an early draft and gave good suggestions.

The following reviewers made many helpful suggestions, for which I am grateful: Andrea Berta, University of Texas, El Paso; Marlene Ferris, VWR International; Ron Lennon, Barry University; Barbara Limbach, Chadron State College; Dona Orr, Boise State University; and William Rothwell, Penn State University.

Finally, my wife, Ann, provided companionship and encouragement, but she also made certain I focused on more than just writing this book. She makes life fun and deserves special thanks.

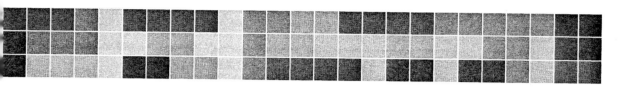

About the Author

John Kline is a professional motivational speaker living in Montgomery, Alabama. He is also professor and Director of the Institute for Leadership Development at Troy State University.

Dr. Kline grew up in Iowa, graduated from the Iowa State University with a B.S. in English and Speech, received Master's and Ph.D. degrees in Speech Communication from the University of Iowa, and completed post-doctoral study at Harvard University.

He has been a professor at the University of New Mexico, the University of Missouri–Columbia, and the United States Air Force Air University, where he gained a reputation as the Air Force's leading expert on public speaking. Businesses and corporations call him often to train personnel to speak and listen more effectively. Dr. Kline has another book in the NetEffect series titled *Listening Effectively: Achieving High Standards in Communication.*

Visit his website at www.klinespeak.com.

Introduction

READER: IT'S WORTH YOUR TIME TO READ THIS PAGE

An objective is given at the start of each chapter describing what you should learn from the chapter. More specifically, you are asked to do one of the following:

- Know—remember and recognize things you learn in the chapter
- Comprehend—translate, interpret, and extrapolate what you learn to new situations (different presentations)
- Apply—use what you learn in preparing and presenting presentations

Tasks are also given at the start of each chapter. Accomplishing these tasks demonstrates that you have achieved the objective. You will soon discover that these chapter objectives are similar to objectives you will design for your own presentations—although you may want to use different words than *know, comprehend,* and *apply.* To judge the effectiveness of your presentations, you may develop tasks to measure listener behavior, just as I have done in this book.

Best wishes! You are now ready to begin. This book will help you become a better speaker.

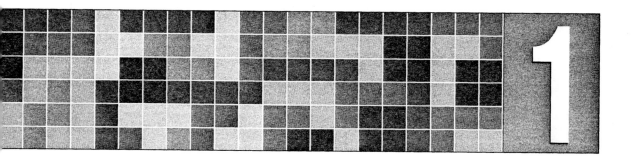

Preparing to Speak

OBJECTIVE

- To know the necessary steps before you organize, support, and make a presentation

TASKS

- Explain the importance of knowing about the speaking situation and your audience.

- Tell how to choose and narrow your subject.

- Differentiate among presentations to inform, to persuade, and to entertain.

- Explain what TOOTSIFELT means and how it can help your presentation be listener centered.

- Differentiate among briefings, lectures, and speeches.

- Explain the procedure for gathering material for your presentation.

Do you get nervous and fearful even *thinking* about the prospect of giving a speech or presentation? If so, you're not alone. Speaking in front of a group is the greatest fear of most people. It ranks ahead of the fear of dying, riding in an airplane, or failure in other areas of life.

You may be unsure of your own speaking ability. But there is good news. You can be an effective speaker, the kind others admire—the kind who gets the job done in every speaking situation. This book will enable you to meet this objective. It's simply a matter of mastering basic techniques and principles of preparing and presenting that have been learned and used successfully by thousands of speakers.

INSIGHT   *"People are afraid of public speaking. . . . In fact most say it's their number one fear. Death, apparently, only comes second."*

—Jerry Seinfeld

ANALYZE THE SITUATION AND THE AUDIENCE

Know as much about the situation and audience as you can before you prepare your presentation. Many of the things to consider will be covered later in this book, but here is a checklist to get you started:

- What's the occasion?
- Who will the audience be?
- How many are expected to attend?
- Where will I speak?
- What time do I begin?
- What does my audience expect of me?
- How can I gain and hold their attention?
- How should I organize my presentation?
- What kind of supporting material should I use for my ideas?
- What kind of language or cultural differences might exist?
- Will there be a question-and-answer period?
- Will audience members interrupt with questions?
- How long should my talk last?
- If I start late, am I still expected to end at a certain time?
- Am I supposed to speak on a certain subject, or is the choice mine?
- What does this audience already know about my subject?
- Will I be able to use visual aids? If so, what type will work best?
- How will the audience be dressed?

- How should I dress?
- Will I be standing behind a lectern?
- Will I be using a microphone? What kind? Cordless? Handheld?
- If I drive to the place, where will I park?
- Will somebody meet me?
- Who will introduce me? Does this person need information from me?

These are just a few of the questions you will want answered. Certainly the most important ones deal with your audience and your relationship to them.

Nothing contributes more to the success of a talk than knowing about your audience and fitting your presentation to them. Nothing leads to failure more than not doing so. Talking to hear your own voice may feed your ego, but it doesn't help you achieve the goal of communicating with your audience. The basic premise of this book is that *all presentations should be listener centered*. Therefore, you should know as much about your audience as possible. Take time to analyze them before preparing your speech. Who are they? What are their likes and dislikes? What do you know about them? What can you find out? Remember, the more you know about your audience, the better job you will do speaking to them.

All presentations should be listener centered.	**INSIGHT**

Audience Analysis

Two reliable methods can be used to gain information about audiences. Used together, they are extremely helpful.

First, think about what you already know about the audience. Perhaps you have talked to this audience before, or perhaps you have talked to similar ones. Knowing such demographic variables as age, gender, socioeconomic status, religion, educational attainment, and experience of audience members will help you relate your message to them. If one or more important variables separate you from the audience, give special attention to ways of emphasizing similarities and reducing differences.

Second, if you haven't talked to the audience before, talk with someone who has. Perhaps a friend or colleague has talked to them and can tell you what to expect. I once spoke to a club that regularly interrupted and heckled guest speakers—even ones they liked. Fortunately, I had been forewarned. Granted, this audience behavior is extreme and perhaps even improper. Still, it's better to know about such things before you speak. Stop, take inventory of what you already know about the audience, and then find out more from someone who is more familiar with them.

Over the past three decades, I have talked to many audiences—old and young, rural and urban, American and international, military and civilian, middle-class and wealthy, homogeneous and diverse. I have often talked on the same subjects to very different audiences. I learned long ago that it's worth my effort and time to know all I can about the audience. This knowledge allows me to make necessary adjustments—to emphasize certain things, rearrange parts, or change a story here and there. Always keep the audience in mind.

At times, even experienced speakers do poorly because they don't know their audience and are not wise enough to adjust to it. Recently, a national television personality spoke on a college campus in a southern city. He gave the same speech he had given with much success on other college campuses. Unfortunately, he didn't learn what he needed to know about his audience on this campus. Some of his material was "off-color" and inappropriate for the very conservative campus where he was speaking. Even when he saw that he was offending the audience, however, he didn't adjust. He bombed out. Some people walked out during his speech, and the applause at the end was polite at best.

INSIGHT *Always respect your audience. If you aren't sure whether your material is appropriate, play it safe—don't use it.*

One old-time comedian often told stories to one audience that might be inappropriate for another. But he was able to adjust to the audience. He started his comedy routine by telling his audience five different types of one-liner jokes. Audience reaction let him know if the audience was in the mood for silly humor, political humor, or blue jokes. Then he simply adjusted his routine to what would be effective for the particular audience that night. Experienced speakers know their audience and are wise enough to adjust.

INSIGHT *"The difference between a smart man and a wise man is that a smart man knows what to say; a wise man knows whether or not to say it."*

—Frank M. Garafola

Audience Attitude

Learning various demographic characteristics of an audience and adapting to them are usually fairly easy. Information about the projected size of the audience and place you will speak is simple to obtain. But audience attitude toward the subject of the speech and the speaker are often more difficult to determine. Yet both are important to the success of the speech. Later, this chapter discusses how to select a subject—one that suits your purpose and your audience. Later in the book, you will learn how speakers can enhance their credibility with the audience, through both the supporting material they use and their delivery.

At times, speakers may face unfriendly audiences. A CEO of a company that has just sustained substantial losses confronts a group of angry stockholders; a boss tells his employees that for the second straight year there will be no raises; or a spokesperson says her company will not pay for damages consumers claimed were caused by the company's product. In such circumstances, the audience's emotions make effective communication difficult. The first task for the speaker is to change audience attitude—if not to friendliness, then at least to a more neutral position. Your chances for success are much greater if you build rapport with your listeners. The following techniques can help you.

1. *Avoid behaving in a conceited or antagonistic manner.* Don't turn off your audience by acting as if you have all the answers. Audiences also turn off to speakers who appear self-centered or hostile. On the other hand, they warm up to someone who appears cordial and conciliatory.

"Conceit is God's gift to little men."	
—Bruce Barton	

2. *Demonstrate a genuine concern for your listeners by talking about things that concern them and by talking at their level.* All speaking should be listener centered. Audiences will react much more favorably if they believe a speaker has the audience's best interests at heart.

3. *Smile.* Show friendliness and warmth toward your listeners. Audiences like speakers better who smile and come across as friendly, warm human beings.

A smile is the shortest distance between two people.	**INSIGHT**

4. *Emphasize similarities between your listeners and you.* It's no secret that audiences relate better to speakers who are similar to them. Knowing this, effective speakers accentuate similarities they have with the audience. For example, with rural audiences, I highlight the fact that I grew up on a farm; with religious groups, I refer to my faith; and with military audiences,

I mention my military experience. Even if you don't have firsthand experience, search for ways to reduce perceived differences between you and your audience. Remember, you can always relate to them as human beings with whom you share many of the same values.

5. *Be honest and straightforward.* First, in a free society, integrity is highly valued. Second, nothing angers or antagonizes an audience more than its belief that speakers are not being honest or are withholding information that they could and should share. Third, it is the right thing to do. Honesty really is the best policy, and it enhances your credibility with the audience.

6. *If you use humor, use good taste.* Consider the age, gender, beliefs, and values of the audience. Also, be very careful in making audience members targets of your humor. Humor at your own expense is especially effective—audiences generally like people who can laugh at themselves. Chapter 5 discusses how to use humor effectively.

7. *Indicate your association with people who are experts on the subject and are held in high esteem by the audience.* But do this only if it adds to the talk. Simply dropping names has a negative effect on most audiences.

8. *Don't let negative, nonverbal aspects of your behavior contradict what you say.* In other words, your audience will judge you not only by what you say but by how you sound and look saying it. Aim for a positive image or effect every time you speak.

9. *Demonstrate that you are an expert and have done your homework on the subject.* Preparation is always essential, but it's especially important when facing a hostile audience. Speakers turn off audiences when they don't seem to know what they're talking about, especially if audiences are hostile to the speaker.

10. *Consider not stating the main idea or conclusion at the outset.* First, present the facts your audience accepts; then build toward your conclusion. That is, if you believe the audience is predisposed to disagree with the conclusion, lead up to it with solid facts and rational arguments.

Most audiences will be friendly. They consist of people favorably disposed toward you as a speaker. Most people want you to do a good job. Furthermore, they usually don't strongly disagree with your point of view. An informative presentation to other members of your organization, a speech to a local civic club, and a classroom report are examples of speaking before friendly audiences.

| INSIGHT | *Speaking might be easier if it weren't for the audience.* |

Exercise	Audience Differences

Compare two or more different audiences, such as a specific college class, a political action group, a group of friends, or an organization you either belong to or know about. Choose a subject and pretend you're going to speak to each group on that subject. Look again at the list given earlier in this chapter. Also consider relevant variables, including age, gender, socio-economic status, educational attainment, experience, and attitude toward your subject. How do the groups differ on these and other variables? How would you most likely adapt your presentation for each group?

CHOOSE THE RIGHT SUBJECT

Selecting a subject for a presentation should be easy, but sometimes it seems difficult—especially when students are trying to choose a subject for a speech class. On the job, or in the community, you seldom have to look for something to talk about. The subjects are implicit in the organizations. For example, a presentation or briefing at work arises from the need to communicate certain subject matter. Even in teaching, a lecture is presented to satisfy a particular curriculum need. On the other hand, a speech to a local civic club or business group may provide you with more latitude in selecting the subject—unless, of course, you are asked to address a club or group on a particular subject. When given the choice, how do you select the subject?

Selecting the Subject

Obviously, you'll want to speak on something you know about. But the subject of the presentation will also depend on the group. You most likely wouldn't address a local group of restaurant owners about recent advances in mortuary science. Nor would you talk to morticians about ways to make a salad look more appetizing. Be listener centered; think about the audience you will be speaking to. Then choose an appropriate subject and treatment of the subject. Even if you have been asked to speak on a certain subject, you will usually be free to choose the particular aspect of the subject to emphasize. Ask yourself several questions about the subject:

1. *Is this the best subject?* This question may pose a challenge, but you can answer more wisely if you consider several different subjects. A carefully selected subject or aspect of the subject chosen after some thought will be better than the "straw-clutching" effect that characterizes the way many people choose their subjects.

2. *Do I know a lot about this subject—and can I find out more?* If not, then it isn't a good subject. There's no substitute for deep, authoritative knowledge of the subject.

3. *Am I interested in the subject?* If you're not interested, preparation will be a dull task, and you'll have difficulty capturing audience interest. Talking about a community service project that you have worked on or discussing a new program that you helped implement is probably much closer to your heart than speaking on a subject you found while searching through a list of suggested topics.

4. *Is the subject suitable for my audience?* Will they understand? Will they be interested? A subject may be suitable or interesting to an audience if it vitally concerns their well-being, offers solutions to their problems, is new or timely, or involves a conflict of opinion.

5. *Can the subject or aspect of the subject be discussed adequately in the time available?* Many speakers fail to narrow their subject. Therefore, they generally do one of two things: (1) they don't adequately cover the subject, or (2) they talk too long. Both results are bad.

INSIGHT	*Often, the hardest part of giving a talk is coming up with the right subject.*

Narrowing the Subject

Some subjects are too broad or complex to be adequately covered in a single presentation. In 10 or 20 minutes, you can't tell much about "Government in the United States," but perhaps you can adequately cover "The Legislative Branch of Federal Government," or "How a Bill Becomes a Law." Speakers often tackle subjects that are too broad. You can pare a big topic down to size by moving from general to specific. The general and abstract topic "Education," for example, may be successfully narrowed to the more concrete and specific "New Standards for Teacher Training in the United States." Here are the steps followed in limiting this subject:

- Education (much too abstract)
- Education in the U.S. (not much better)
- Higher Education in the U.S. (a beginning in the right direction)
- Colleges of Education in the U.S. (a little more specific)
- Teacher Training Programs in the U.S. (something concrete)
- Standards for Teacher Training Programs in the U.S. (getting better)
- New Standards for Teacher Training in the U.S. (a suitable topic)

Limit your subject in terms of your own interests and qualifications, your listeners' needs and demands, and the time allotted to your presentation.

Exercise   Narrowing Your Subject

Following the example given above on how the broad subject "Education" was narrowed to the more suitable topic "New Standards for Teacher Training in the United States," give the steps you might go through in narrowing the following topics for a 10- to 20-minute speech on each of the following: Multiculturalism in America, Terrorism in the World Today, Economic Conditions of the Twentieth Century, Corporate America, and the American Way of Life. Explain why you limited each subject the way you did.

Choosing a Title That Fits

The title is a specific label given to the presentation, an advertising slogan or catchword that captures the spirit of the talk and tantalizes the potential audience. Generally, the exact phrasing of the title is not decided until the presentation has been built. At other times, it may come to mind as you work on the presentation. At still other times, it may come early and guide your planning. An effective title should be relevant, provocative, and brief.

But don't mislead your listeners. Don't include words in the title merely to get attention if they have no relevance to the presentation itself. "The Eleventh Commandment" is a relevant title for a speech that addresses the fact that the commandment "Thou shall not get caught" has seemed to replace some of the other commandments. "A Pat on the Back, A Punch in the Mouth" is certainly a more provocative title than "How Positive and Negative Reinforcement Affects Our Children." "You Cannot *Not* Communicate" is briefer and more provocative than "The Impossibility of Failing to Communicate."

The preceding three titles are all catchy and suitable for speeches or presentations to certain groups. But in the business and corporate world, the direct approach usually works best. A briefing or training session on effective listening might simply be titled "Effective Listening." For that matter, "Listening Effectively"—a title of another book in this Prentice Hall NetEffect Series—may be even better because the first word, *listening*, grabs attention better than the word *effective*. Good titles are descriptive but should also be inviting. Attention should be piqued so the audience wants to listen. Good titles gain listeners' attention.

"I didn't go. I knew from the title it would be bad."

INSIGHT

—student telling why he didn't attend a lecture for extra credit

DECIDE ON YOUR PURPOSE

Once you have your audience and subject in mind, decide on your purpose. The three general purposes of speaking are to inform, to persuade, and to entertain. All speaking has at least one of these purposes; many have two, and some, all three.

To Inform

Informative presentations expand the knowledge and understanding of the audience. The purpose is not to urge listeners to believe a certain way or take a certain action; nor is it primarily to entertain. The purpose is to communicate a message and provide information.

Sometimes informative talks involve demonstration. For example, a presenter speaking on "Illusion in Magic" may demonstrate some of the concepts he is discussing. A state official may speak concerning a program in which parents make regular contributions toward a guaranteed college education for their young children. During the speech, the official projects a PowerPoint image of the form parents must complete and then she demonstrates how to fill it out. An informative speech that uses PowerPoint slides or other visual aids involves demonstration.

Informative presentations often explain things. For instance, the head of the power company may speak to the Rotary Club, explaining reasons for an increase in the cost of electricity to local businesses. Your boss may ask you to make a presentation about a project at a staff meeting. At the start of a new class, an instructor may ask students to give three- to five-minute "get acquainted" speeches about themselves. At other times, teachers explain the way students are to prepare assignments or perform tasks. These are all examples of explanation in informative speaking.

Reports are another kind of informative presentation. A company may send employees to a national conference. When they return, they are expected to give an oral report to other members of the organization explaining what they experienced. A teacher may ask students to give book reports. A chairperson or leader may ask for committee reports. Reports provide information.

Whatever form presentations take—demonstrations, explanations, reports, or some combination of the three—the purpose is to inform. Informative talks help the audience understand information.

To Persuade

A persuasive speech or presentation is designed to move an audience to belief or action on some topic, product, or other matter. Military recruiting speeches to high school graduating classes, presentations to management urging financial support for a proposed project, sales presentations, and sermons are all primarily talks to persuade.

While all speech may have a persuasive element, true persuasion attempts to influence attitudes or actions. Smokers are persuaded to become non-smokers, civilians are persuaded to join the military, shoppers are persuaded to become buyers, church attendees are persuaded to become members, the undecided are persuaded to take a stand or position, and people are persuaded to change their attitude about some matter either important or trivial. Some of these responses are more drastic than others, but each seeks to influence an attitude or promote an action.

Sometimes the speaker does not seek a change but wants merely to begin to shape a response. That is, the speaker wants to predispose listeners toward the desired response or at least cause them to be open-minded about it. This approach may work well if the audience has no real opinion and little knowledge about a topic. The approach is also a good one to use when the audience holds an opinion that is firmly opposed to that of the speaker—a situation in which little chance of a drastic change exists. Experienced speakers know the wisdom of shaping or attempting to move the audience incrementally toward the desired response rather than attempting to promote a drastic shift.

At still other times, speakers may want to reinforce an existing opinion or provide support for a current behavior. Priests, rabbis, and ministers often reinforce their congregants' beliefs and support the status quo. Parents reinforce family values and beliefs for their children. Whether seeking to change, shape, or reinforce, persuasion always involves an attempt to influence action, attitudes, or both.

Which should a speaker attempt to influence, attitudes or actions (behaviors)? It depends, but generally speakers attempt to influence attitudes so that the desired behavior will follow. Changing behavior without changing attitudes usually requires coercion. For example, a supervisor may coerce, or force, an employee to act a certain way. The action has been influenced, at least temporarily, but the attitude has not. Without a change in attitude, the employee may or may not act the same way when the supervisor is absent. It will probably depend upon the respect—or fear—the employee has for authority and for the supervisor. Even if the employee consistently follows the directives of a supervisor, that employee may be thinking, "If I had my way, I'd do things differently." On the other hand, if the employee believes—has the attitude—that the action the supervisor wants is good, the desired behavior is a natural consequence.

To Entertain

Entertaining speaking is the most difficult type for most persons to master, yet it is the type of speaking at which most people wish they excelled. Bringing pleasure to an audience provides real satisfaction.

We could argue that all presentations—informative, persuasive, and entertaining—should be pleasurable. We could also contend that both informative and persuasive talks should have entertainment value. But unlike either informative or persuasive presentations, the *primary* purpose of an entertaining presentation or speech is just that: to entertain, delight, amuse. Often, of course, speakers seek to inform or persuade audiences while entertaining them. While there are different types of entertaining speeches, perhaps the most common is the after-dinner speech. After-dinner speeches are often given primarily to entertain. Of course, some speakers fail.

INSIGHT	*"I have just got a new theory of eternity."* —Albert Einstein after listening to an after-dinner speech

Entertaining speeches often rely upon concrete examples, dramatic anecdotes, vivid comparisons, clever exaggeration, witty phrasing, and stories with unexpected endings. Humor is one of the main tools of speakers who seek to entertain. Effective speakers use humor to the best of their ability. But they must be careful not to overrate their ability. Most speakers should not compete with the comedian. Chapter 5 discusses the use of humor in speaking.

Exercise   What's the Speaker's Purpose?

Which of the following would most likely have a purpose to inform? To persuade? To entertain? Give your reasons for each choice.

- Report on a conference to a group of office colleagues
- Prosecuting attorney's final summation before a jury
- Roast of a prominent community leader to her peers
- Method to be used in filling out the new travel voucher
- Lecture to a college class on the three major purposes of speaking
- Briefing to an organization on the major elements of a new plan
- Adolescent's plea to his parents for extending curfew
- Presentation to a legislative body advocating legalization of marijuana
- Talk to a travel club on the greatest places to visit in Tuscany

Of course, in some cases, more than one purpose may be appropriate. But this exercise should help you think about having a purpose in mind when you speak. For further practice, listen critically to the next presentations you hear—lectures, speeches on television or radio, briefings at work, or even conversations at home or with friends—and determine the speaker's purpose.

The general purposes—to inform, to persuade, or to entertain—will influence how you organize, support, and deliver your talk. Still, the basic principles and techniques covered in the following chapters apply to all presentations. Learn them and you'll be a successful speaker/presenter in any situation—work, professional meetings, social gatherings, clubs, classes, and just about anywhere a group is gathered. But before you begin to prepare your presentation, you must determine your central idea and decide on a specific objective.

STATE A SPECIFIC OBJECTIVE

Your purposes for speaking influence how you approach the task and the general response you want from the audience. An informative presentation seeks audience understanding. A persuasive presentation seeks a change in attitudes or behavior. An entertaining presentation seeks to divert, amuse, or in some way give the listeners pleasure. On the other hand, your *central idea* identifies the essence of your message and is captured in your objective. *Your objective tells the specific response you want from your audience—what you expect them to know (or think), feel, or do as a result of listening to you.* Objectives do not state what the speaker is to do; purposes do that. Rather, they state the response the speaker desires from listeners after the speech. This is important: It's not what you, the speaker, want to do; it's what you want each listener to think, feel, or do after hearing you speak.

Don't merely think about your objectives. Write them down. The method I will describe for doing this may seem silly, but it works. Start this way. "The *objective of this speech is for each listener to . . .* " (TOOTSIFELT). Then finish the sentence with what you want them to think, feel or do. The key is TOOTSIFELT (pronounced: Tootsie felt—as in "Tootsie felt happy" or "Tootsie felt good"). Write every speech or presentation objective with TOOTSIFELT, and you will have properly stated objectives, the kind that will help you focus on the audience.

TOOTSIFELT is the key to good objectives.   **INSIGHT**

Of course you may want more than one response from your audience. You may want them to feel or believe that candidate Jones is the most qualified, and you may also want them to cast their vote for Jones. In this case, your central idea is that Jones is the best candidate. Your overriding objective is for them to vote for Jones. Therefore, your objective would be stated this way: "The objective of this speech is for each listener to vote for Jones." Or, "TOOTSIFELT vote for Jones." *Your objective is* not *for you to tell them why Jones is the best candidate.* That may be your task, but it's not your objective. *Your objective is what you want* their response *to be.* It's what you want them to know, feel, or do.

The *central idea* for this book is that it is important for people to be able to speak effectively. Therefore, the *objective* of this book is for each reader to be able to prepare and present speeches, lectures, and briefings effectively. That's it! Nothing else. The objective is not for me to write about how to speak. That's my task, but it's not my objective. If I do the task well, I will meet my objective.

At this point, you should understand the relationship among subjects, general purposes, and specific objectives. Although the following three examples are very simple, they illustrate these relationships. The same principles apply to business, educational, and training contexts. Pay special attention to each TOOTSIFELT.

Subject/Title:	From Iowa to the Air Force
General Purpose:	To entertain
Specific Objective:	TOOTSIFELT enjoy the humor of a young man making the transition from an Iowa farm to the Air Force.
Subject/Title:	You cannot *not* communicate
General Purpose:	To inform
Specific Objective:	TOOTSIFELT understand that we constantly communicate messages verbally and nonverbally whether we mean to or not.
Subject/Title:	Equality for all
General Purpose:	To persuade
Specific Objective:	TOOTSIFELT dedicate themselves anew to the principle of racial and social equality for all.

Once you understand your audience, have the subject, know the general purpose, and state the specific objective or TOOTSIFELT, one consideration remains before you begin to gather material and organize it for delivery. What type of presentation do you plan to give?

Exercise	Why TOOTSIFELT?

Tell what the letters in TOOTSIFELT stand for.

Now rewrite each of these objectives correctly using TOOTSIFELT:

- Tell ways to increase the profit margin in our company.
- Inform of the probable changes in next year's business environment.
- Talk about how to raise rabbits for profit.
- Persuade my listeners to contribute to the relief fund.
- Entertain my listeners with stories from my summer vacation.
- Explain the benefits of the European Common Market.
- Inform my audience how to save money by buying on-line.
- Tell my listeners why they should vote to increase property taxes.

PLAN THE RIGHT TYPE OF PRESENTATION

Although briefings, lectures, and speeches are each often referred to by the generic titles *speech*, *talk*, or *presentation*, differences exist among the three types. These differences will influence your organization, support, beginning, ending, and delivery. *Briefings* present information quickly and concisely. *Lectures* are used to teach new material. *Speeches* are given in a variety of situations.

Briefings

Briefings originated in military settings. Seeing their value for presenting much information, former military members introduced briefings into business settings. Today, briefings are the most common type of presentation in both settings. Sometimes their purpose is to inform—to tell about a mission, project, operation, or concept. At times, they enable listeners to perform a procedure or carry out instructions. At other times, they advocate or seek to persuade listeners to accept a certain solution or way of doing things. The ABCs of briefing help us to remember that a briefing should always be Accurate, Brief, and Clear. Accuracy and clarity characterize all good speaking. Brevity is a virtue in much speaking, but it is a requirement for briefings.

"Spartans, stoics, heroes, saints and gods use a short and positive speech." —Ralph Waldo Emerson	**INSIGHT**

The requirement for brevity dictates that you not use extraneous or "nice to know" support. Visual aids are often used to save time and achieve accuracy. Humor is seldom used because entertainment is never a purpose of briefings. Briefings concentrate on the facts. They also generally begin and end according to a prescribed format (discussed in Chapter 7).

Lectures

A workplace marked by change, transformation, reengineering, and re-invention has promoted lifelong learning. No longer is instruction primarily the domain of colleges, universities, and trade schools. Although interactive methods and electronic technology have reshaped education and training, both formal lectures (where the instructor does most of the talking) and informal lectures (characterized by verbal interaction with learners) are still a cornerstone of learning. Although lectures may have secondary purposes to persuade or entertain, their primary purpose is to teach or inform learners about a given subject. Clear organization and the use of factual material help students learn and remember what was taught. But unlike briefings, lectures may use humor and other attention-commanding materials. They may even play to the emotions of the learners, unlike in most briefings. Visual support and visual aids are often used, not only to save time and improve accuracy but also to clarify ideas.

Speeches

Speeches are often categorized by the setting, which may be a civic club, a business luncheon, an academic consortium, or any one of many different contexts. Many business, organization, and academic conferences and conventions feature keynote speeches, whose purpose is often to arouse enthusiasm and present issues of primary interest. After-dinner speeches or luncheon speeches are simply speeches given after dinner or during lunch— perhaps to a civic or social gathering, but often at business conferences. Plenary speeches, which may or may not be keynote or luncheon speeches, require that everyone attending a meeting be present for the speech. Plenary speeches are often given at business meetings and at other organizational gatherings.

In addition to the many speaking situations, any one or a combination of the three purposes may be appropriate. Speeches to inform use the same kind of organization and support materials as lectures. Entertaining speeches may rely heavily on humor and other attention-getting support. Persuasive speeches are characterized by more appeal to emotions or motives than any other kind of talk you will give. Appeal to such motives as fear. curiosity, loyalty, adventure, pride, and sympathy is common in persuasion. The distinction between appeals to logic and appeals to emotion, however, is in content rather than form. Any type of verbal and visual supporting material may be primarily logical or emotional. *But just because support appeals to the emotions does not mean it has to be illogical.* Emotional support may or may not be based on strong logic; logical appeals may or may not appeal to the emotions. (Chapter 4 discusses logic and the use of emotional appeals.)

"The speech belongs half to the speaker and half to the listener."

—Michel de Montaigne

GATHER YOUR MATERIAL

With the general purpose and specific objective in mind, you are ready to gather informative material on the subject. This step is important. To give a good presentation, you need good information. The source for information can be your own experience or the experience of others you obtain through conversation with them, interviews, and written or observed material. You may often draw from all these sources in a single presentation.

The best way to sound like you know what you're talking about is to know what you're talking about.

INSIGHT

Self

The first step in researching an oral presentation is the assembly of personal knowledge you have about the subject. Most people don't speak on subjects they know nothing about, yet many run first to libraries, bookstores, and the Internet for information.

Start with what you already know. Sit down with a piece of paper and pen or at a computer, and write a preliminary or planning outline of the talk you plan to give. (Chapter 2 discusses planning outlines.) This will be time well spent. Such a self-inventory will most likely suggest a tentative organization, and, even more important, it will point out gaps in knowledge where you need to do further research. You'll know what information you need to collect, and you'll get an idea of the kinds of verbal and visual supporting material you will want to include in your talk.

You're going to give the talk. Start with your own knowledge before you look elsewhere. Things from your own experience are easiest to talk about.

Others

The second step in the research process is to draw on the experience of others. People who are interested and knowledgeable on the subject provide many ideas. Talk to them.

The most fruitful source, of course, is the true expert. Sometimes, such experts are easier to contact than you might think. Often, they live or work near you. Other people—teachers, government officials, and community leaders—can help you find these people. But even if the experts aren't nearby, the Internet has made the quick exchange of information possible. You may be surprised at the positive response you'll receive when contacting experts on the Internet. These people can help clarify your thinking, provide facts, and suggest good sources for further research. Suggestions for further sources can help you narrow your search without having to investigate a large bulk of material.

Outside Research

Bookstores, libraries, and the Internet provide an abundance of material. Bookstores may have some of the latest and most carefully researched information, especially if the writer or compiler is an expert who provides footnotes, endnotes, and sources for further research and study. Well-stocked libraries contain books, newspapers, popular magazines, scholarly journals, abstracts, subject files, and microfilms.

The Internet may provide the largest amount of material for your speech. Much of it is very good; much is not. Be cautious when using the Internet as a source of material. Here are several things to keep in mind as you search for material on the Internet to use:

1. Misinformation of five general types often appears.
   a. Unintentional: the person who posted the information just doesn't know
   b. Intentional: false, deliberately deceptive information—hoaxes
   c. False rumors: anecdotal claims that may be partly true or completely false
   d. Junk: flotsam and jetsam of the Internet
   e. Urban legends: popularly believed but false narratives

2. The validity of the source of information is often difficult or impossible to determine—and information is no better than its source. Chapter 4 emphasizes that sources must be both expert (competent in the subject) and trustworthy (worthy of belief). If you can't determine the author's name, position, organizational affiliation, and support for the claims or assertions made, beware! Most valid sources will also tell how to contact them.

3. Information is often outdated. Printed material, such as books and magazine articles, is usually dated, but it's often difficult or impossible to tell

when the material on the Internet was posted or updated. Dating may not be a problem if you are researching the effects of World War I, but it would be a problem if you plan to speak on "The Most Popular Current Urban Legends."

4. Information is often unsubstantiated. Has the writer listed sources, given available corroboration, and provided documentation? Make your goal a source that provides convincing evidence for claims made—a source you can triangulate (find at least two other valid sources that support it).

5. Some information is plagiarized or copied from someone else and then posted on the Internet as one's own idea. In other words, you don't know its origin.

6. Treat material from the Internet as you would material from a book or a journal article. Don't pass it off as your own, and don't quote from it without giving credit where it is due. Consider the accompanying box "Who Wrote It?"

"Who Wrote It?"

Many years ago, I was teaching a night class at a local university. A student handed me a paper he claimed to have written on public speaking. I liked the way it began. These were the first lines:

"Do you get nervous and fearful even *thinking* about the prospect of giving a speech or presentation? If so, you're not alone. Speaking in front of a group is the greatest fear of most people. It ranks ahead of the fear of dying, riding in an airplane, or failure in other areas of life."

"You may be unsure of your own speaking ability. But there is good news. You can be an effective speaker, the kind others admire—the kind who gets the job done in every speaking situation."

I told him "I like the beginning of your paper." Then I asked, "Who wrote it?" He stammered and then said it came from the Internet. He reluctantly showed me where. He had copied it word for word. I explained this was a case of plagiarism even though no author was listed. Furthermore, I told him I knew the author and would prove it. I handed him a copy of a training document I had written some years earlier—one widely distributed throughout the Air Force. Somebody had recently placed my words on the Internet, passing them off as their own. The opening lines of the document I had written were identical to the ones the student had quoted. The student was dumbfounded. (By the way, they are now the opening lines of this chapter.) I showed mercy on the embarrassed student, who learned a valuable lesson. I am sure he thought about it often as he wrote a new paper on a different subject. He has long since graduated and sometime later wrote to thank me both for a valuable lesson and for the compassion I showed him.

EVALUATE YOUR MATERIAL

The final step in the research process is to evaluate the material gathered. Here you step back from all the material you've assembled. You may find that you have more than enough material—perhaps enough for several presentations.

You must decide which material to use, which to file for later use, and which you can dispose of. Although we will discuss the use of both verbal and visual supporting material in later chapters, ask yourself some preliminary questions as you begin to decide which material to use:

1. Does it support my general purpose—to inform, to persuade, or to entertain?
2. Does it support my specific objective—the TOOTSIFELT?
3. Will it fit well with one of my main points or subpoints?
4. Will it appeal to my audience?
5. Can it be used easily?
6. Is it appropriate?

Now you're at a crucial point—the point where you must organize to speak. You may have a tentative organization in mind for your main points, and perhaps even for subpoints. Now is the time to finalize the organization pattern and make certain that the main points are organized to support the central purpose, specific objective, and general purpose of the presentation. The time spent ensuring that your talk is well organized will pay off. Good organization will help you present the information to your listeners and help them understand what you are saying. The next chapter presents the six major patterns of organization and strategies to use with each pattern. But first check what you have learned so far.

Check Yourself: What Have You Learned?

- ☐ Public speaking is the greatest fear of most people.
- ☐ The first step in preparing is to analyze your speaking situation and your audience.
- ☐ All presentations should be listener centered.
- ☐ Narrow the subject to fit the audience and the time.
- ☐ The three general purposes of speaking are to inform, to persuade, and to entertain.
- ☐ State specific objectives using TOOTSIFELT to ensure they are listener centered.
- ☐ When gathering material, start with yourself, then others, and finally look to outside sources.
- ☐ The Internet is a great source of material, but be careful to confirm the material's validity.
- ☐ Evaluate your material to see if it fits your purpose, objective, and audience.

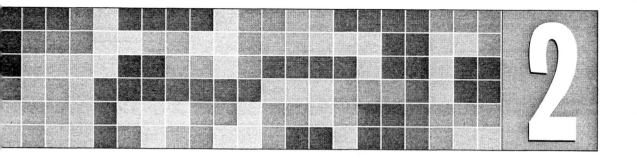

Organizing the Presentation

OBJECTIVE

- To comprehend appropriate patterns and strategies used to organize presentations

TASKS

- Give examples of presentations that use each of the patterns of organization given in this chapter.

- Tell how different strategies might be used with each pattern.

- Explain how different patterns of organization may be used within the same presentation.

- Demonstrate how to construct a planning outline.

Clear organization is vital to effective speaking. The organization must fit the subject, purpose (to inform, to persuade, to entertain), and objective of the presentation—the TOOTSIFELT discussed in Chapter 1. Above all, organization must meet the needs of the listeners. This means that the *main points must be organized to logically support the central idea of your presentation, which you have captured in the objective.* Speaking is a listener-centered activity.

Many speakers fail to consider the audience adequately when organizing their talks. Speakers have the responsibility for leading listeners mentally from where they are at the beginning of a speech or presentation to where they are to be at the end. The message must be organized with listeners in mind; the organization should conform to their thinking processes and expectations.

> **INSIGHT** *Main points must be organized to logically support the central idea of your presentation, which you have captured in the objective.*

Each briefing, lecture, or speech needs an introduction, a body, and a conclusion. In most instances, the introduction and conclusion should be prepared after the body of the talk, since the material in the body can serve as a guide for preparing these. This chapter tells how to organize the body of the talk. Later, we will discuss how to begin and end.

The first consideration in planning the body of a talk is how to organize the main points and important subpoints. Effective organization of the main points and subpoints will help both you, the speaker, and your audience remember the material—you, while speaking; your audience, after listening.

> **INSIGHT** *"The only way he can grapple with it at all is by first reducing it to a fixed and formal organization."*
>
> —H. L. Menken, *The American Language*, 1921

Most oral presentations, regardless of length, can be divided into two to five main points. Five is usually the maximum number of points from one talk that listeners can be expected to remember. Of course, some talks may have more points. For example, a speech on "Six Sensational Spots in Seattle" would most likely have six points, whereas some short talks might have just one main point. Generally aim for your presentations to have from two to five points. Most listeners have trouble remembering over four or five points. Three points is optimal.

Six useful ways or patterns to organize the main points or subpoints of a talk are by time, space, cause/effect, problem/solution, pro/con, and topic. This chapter illustrates these six patterns and the different strategies that can be used with each. Most of the examples or illustrations given are quite simple, but the same techniques apply to business presentations or those in classrooms or society.

TIME

Our vocabularies are filled with words that refer to time: *now, tomorrow, yesterday, today, sooner, later, earlier, next (last) week (month, year, time)*. We work, play, sleep, and eat at certain times. Major events in our lives are organized by time: births, engagements, marriages, deaths. The time, or chronological, pattern of organization is a natural way to arrange events by the order in which they happened. This pattern also is useful in giving directions that should be followed sequentially. Certain processes, procedures, or historical movements and developments can often be explained best with a time-sequence organizational pattern.

The medical technician discussing mouth-to-mouth resuscitation would probably use a time order for the main points: (1) preliminary steps in preparing the body—proper position, mouth open, tongue and jaw forward; (2) the mouth-to-mouth process; (3) caring for the patient once breathing resumes. Time order is also a logical approach for talks dealing with such subjects as "How to Pack a Parachute," "Development of the Computer," or "How to Prepare a Speech." Furthermore, any talk on a subject with several phases lends itself well to the time pattern. For example, a talk whose objective is for the audience to know that the common market was originally planned to develop in three phases might have the following as its main points: (1) phase one, a customs union where nations agreed to reduce duties; (2) phase two, an economic union allowing laborers and goods to move freely across national borders; and (3) phase three, a political union with national representatives as members of a common parliament and using a common currency.

Rather than looking forward in time from a given moment, you might use the strategy of looking backward. In other words, you might move from a recent time to an earlier time rather than from early to late. Regardless of which strategy you use—early to late, or late to early—the flow of the talk and the transitions from one point to the next should make the chronological relationship between the main points clear to the audience.

Consider the simple outline shown here for a speech on "Raising a Garden." Notice that the four main points are organized chronologically, or by time, following the strategy of going from the earliest time, or first step, to the later times, or second, third, and fourth steps. Notice also how the points support the general purpose and specific objective.

Time Pattern—Early to Late Strategy

Subject/Title:	Raising a Garden
Purpose:	To inform
Objective:	TOOTSIFELT know the basic steps in raising a garden.
Main Points:	I. Prepare the soil.
	II. Plant the seeds.
	III. Cultivate the crops.
	IV. Harvest the produce.

Now look at the outline for the presentation "From Flunky to Boss." This talk also uses the time pattern, but the strategy is reversed. The speaker plans to start with her most recent job and then move backward in time. She is using the late to early strategy. Often, persons filling out job applications are asked to list their employment history starting with the most recent job held then working backward in time. This would be another example of moving back in time.

Time Pattern—Late to Early Strategy

Subject/Title:	From Flunky to Boss
Purpose:	To inform and to entertain
Objective:	TOOTSIFELT see the humor of my different jobs in banking.
Main Points:	I. 2003: Manager—Acting like I know what I'm doing
	II. 2000–2003: Assistant Manager—Learning the secret handshake
	III. 1999–2000: Internal Auditor—Wearing the Black Hat
	IV. 1998–1999: Bank Teller—Finding my way around

SPACE

A spatial or geographical pattern can be very effective in describing relationships. When using this pattern, the talk is developed according to some directional strategy, such as east to west or north to south. For instance, if a speaker were describing the mid-twentieth-century domino theory of Communist infiltration, the strategy might be to arrange the main points according to the geographical locations of various nations and how they would be affected by such infiltration within their geographical region.

With talks on certain objects, the strategy might be to arrange the main points from top to bottom or bottom to top. A fire extinguisher might be described from top to bottom, an organizational chart from the highest-ranking individuals to the lowest ones in the organization, or a library according to the services found on the first floor, then the second, and finally the third.

Sometimes, the strategy is to organize the talk from the center to the outside. For example, the control panel in an airplane might be discussed by first describing those often used instruments in the center, then by moving out toward the surrounding instruments, which are used least often.

With time, the pattern is usually clear. Spatial organization may not be readily apparent to the audience. You, as speaker, should make certain your audience understands how you have organized your talk. Provide necessary elaboration and clarification of how the points relate to one another. A simple listing of the various objects or places without elaboration may confuse listeners.

Consider two outlines, each employing spatial organization—one using a traditional east-to-west strategy; the other, a quite different "spiral" one.

Spatial Pattern—East-to-West Strategy	
Subject/Title:	Year-End Sales Report
Purpose:	To inform
Objective:	TOOTSIFELT know the composite sales for the past year.
Main Points:	I. Sales in the Eastern states
	II. Sales in the Middle states
	III. Sales in the Western states

The organization of the "Year-End Sales Report" speech is clear. The listener will readily understand that the main points are the geographically

Spatial Pattern—Spiral Strategy

Subject/Title: Amos and the Funnel of Fire

Purpose: To inform

Objective: TOOTSIFELT understand judgments prophesied by Amos.

Main Points:

I. Judgment on Damascus

II. Judgment on Gaza

III. Judgment on Tyre

IV. Judgment on Edom

V. Judgment on Ammon

VI. Judgment on Moab

VII. Judgment on Judah

VIII. Judgment on Israel

determined sales regions. The organization of the lecture "Amos and the Funnel of Fire" is not as clear. Most likely, only religious scholars or mideastern geographers would readily understand why the speech was organized this way. An ancient prophet named Amos predicted judgment on eight nations: Damascus, Gaza, Tyre, Edom, Ammon, Moab, Judah, and Israel. From the diagram in Figure 2.1, we see Amos was spiraling, or "funneling," from the outside in. Most likely, the person giving this talk would want to use a visual aid or a map to make the organization clear to listeners.

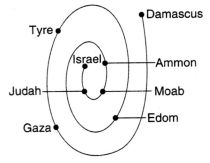

FIGURE 2.1 Amos and the funnel of fire.

CAUSE/EFFECT

A causal pattern of arrangement is used in a talk where one set of conditions is given as a cause for another set. In such talks, one of two basic strategies may be used to arrange points. With a cause/effect strategy, you begin with a given set of conditions and contend that these will produce or have already produced certain results or effects; with an effect/cause strategy, you take a certain set of conditions as the effects and allege that they resulted from certain causes.

The cause/effect strategy might be used, for example, in a talk concerning the increasing number of women in corporate management. The talk might first discuss the fact that women are now assuming more responsible leadership roles in corporations. One effect of women assuming such roles might be that women are now entering the corporate world in increasing numbers rather than joining the ranks of fields that have traditionally attracted women.

The effect/cause strategy might be used, for example, in a talk on child abuse. The first point might explain the effects of child abuse on the children themselves, on the parents, and even on society. The second point might allege that the causes are that the parents themselves were abused as children or that proper parenting education was not received.

Whichever strategy you use, keep in mind these two cautions. (1) *Beware of false causes.* Just because one event or circumstance precedes another does not mean that the former causes the latter. Many persons assume that "first A happened, then B took place, so A must have caused B." (2) *Beware of single causes.* Few things result from a single cause. Many causes are more common, with one playing on another until it is hard to disentangle them. For example, lack of safety features on automobiles is not the only cause of most highway accidents, but this cause, plus careless driving or unsafe highways, may account for many highway accidents.

The two simple outlines here on "Air Pollution" each use a causal pattern or arrangement. One uses the cause/effect strategy; the other, the effect/cause strategy.

Causal Pattern—Cause/Effect Strategy

Subject/Title: Air Pollution

Purpose: To inform

Objective: TOOTSIFELT comprehend the effects of air pollution in cities.

Main Points:

I. Motor vehicles, industrial plants, and private residences discharge large amounts of waste material into the atmosphere. (Cause)

II. This discharge has created serious air pollution in most cities. (Effect)

Causal Pattern—Effect/Cause Strategy

Subject/Title: Air Pollution

Purpose: To inform

Objective: TOOTSIFELT comprehend the causes of air pollution in cities.

Main Points:

    I. Most cities face a serious problem of air pollution. (Effect)

    II. Major causes of this problem are vapors discharged from motor vehicles, industrial plants, and private residences. (Cause)

As seen from the two outlines on air pollution, the objective—which, as always, is listener centered—determines which strategy to use. In the first example, the speaker wants to first inform the audience about the causes of the problem before telling of the effects. In the second example, the speaker chooses to first give the effects before informing the audience of the major causes of air pollution.

PROBLEM/SOLUTION

This pattern presents listeners with a problem and then proposes a way to solve it. With this pattern, you must show a problem exists and then offer corrective action that is (1) practical, (2) desirable, (3) capable of being put into action, and (4) able to solve the problem. The solution also should not introduce worse problems of its own. For example, someone may argue that taxes should be increased to pay for a downtown revitalization project. Opponents may contend that citizens are already overtaxed and that additional taxes would be an undesirable added burden. In other words, the solution to one problem causes a worse problem.

The problem/solution pattern is especially useful when a speaker wants to provide information on which listeners can base decisions. The pattern can also be used effectively with persuasive speeches and lectures in which a speaker wants to present a need or a problem followed by a way or ways to satisfy the need or solve the problem. A problem/solution speech usually has just two points—the first states the problem; the second gives the solution. But different strategies might be used.

One effective strategy is simply referred to as the problem/possible solution/best solution format. That is, first you present the problem. Next, you outline more than one possible solution. Finally, you present the preferred solution. For instance, if the objective is for listeners to comprehend that solar energy is the best solution to the energy crisis, the main points might be as follows: (1) The world is caught in the grip of an energy crisis. (2) Several solutions are possible—increased offshore oil drilling, more nuclear generating plants, more effective harnessing of solar energy. (3) Solar energy is the best long-term solution.

Of course, if listeners already know what the problem and possible solutions are, you may discuss the problem briefly, mention possible solutions, and then spend more time showing why one solution is better than others. Knowing the audience, and knowing what they know, will help you determine the amount of time to spend on each point.

On the other hand, if listeners are not aware or are only slightly aware of the problem or need, you may describe in detail the exact nature of the problem. Sometimes, when listeners become aware of the problem, the solution becomes evident and little time is needed to develop the solution. At other times, you may need time to develop both the problem and the solution, irrespective of which strategy you use.

Still another strategy to use with the problem/solution pattern is to alternate or stagger portions of the problem with portions of the solution. For example, the cost of a project may be seen as one problem, workability as another, time to do the projects as a third. Taking up each portion and, in turn, providing solutions to cost, workability, and time as you present these aspects of the problem may be more helpful to your listeners than if you were to discuss all of the problem and then its total solution.

The three sample outlines shown here each employ different strategies. The first uses the straightforward problem/solution pattern. The next demonstrates the problem/possible solution/best solution strategy. The third shows how the staggered strategy might be used.

Problem/Solution Pattern

Subject/Title:	Johnny May Graduate, but He Still Can't Read
Purpose:	To persuade
Objective:	TOOTSIFELT be committed to get local schools to teach phonetics.
Main Points:	

    I. High school graduates demonstrate a serious reading deficiency.

    II. Teaching phonetics is the solution.

Problem/Solution Pattern—Problem/Possible Solution/Best Solution Strategy

Subject: How to Become a Millionaire

Purpose: To persuade

Objective: TOOTSIFELT believe sound, continued investment is the only sure way to become a millionaire.

Main Points:

    I. Everybody would like to become a millionaire.

    II. There are several ways to become a millionaire, including to

       A. win the lottery.

       B. find the money.

       C. inherit the money.

       D. invest money as you earn it.

    III. The only sure way to become a millionaire is through a sound, continued investment program.

Problem/Solution Pattern—Staggered Strategy

Subject/Title: Total Lifetime Fitness

Purpose: To inform and to persuade

Objective: TOOTSIFELT commit to a program for continued physical, mental, and spiritual fitness (body, mind, and soul).

Main Points:

    I. Problem: Physical fitness requires continual work.

       Solution: Engage in regular aerobic, stretching, and weight-bearing exercise.

    II. Problem: Mental fitness doesn't just happen.

       Solution: Stretch your mind daily with challenging cognitive exercise.

    III. Problem: Spiritual fitness deserves attention.

       Solution: Set aside a time daily for reading, prayer, and meditation.

Whichever strategy you choose, the problem/solution pattern is a good one for persuasive speeches and advocacy briefings. As always, choose the strategy that fits your content and the listener's needs.

PRO/CON

The pro/con pattern, sometimes called the for/against pattern or the advantage/disadvantage pattern, is similar to a problem/ solution pattern in that the talk is often planned to lead to a specific conclusion. However, a major difference is that with the pro/con pattern, fairly even attention is usually directed toward both sides of an issue.

Various strategies can be used with the pro/con pattern. You can start with either the pro side or the con side. Another strategy is known as the *pro/con plus one strategy*. Here speakers give both sides then add a third main point to tell why one side—advantages or disadvantages—is preferable to the other. Also, as with the problem/solution pattern, you might use the stagger strategy, treating the pros and cons of various parts of the issue as you speak.

At times, you must decide whether to present both sides and let listeners draw their own conclusions. You will often want to do this with educated audiences, hostile audiences, and audiences likely to be exposed to counterpersuasion at a later time. At other times, you may want to present both sides, but in such a way that listeners are led to accept the preferred conclusion or the one you want them to accept. For instance, with a talk on the effects of jogging, you may present either advantages or disadvantages first. Then you must decide whether to let listeners make their own decision as to whether one side outweighs the other. Perhaps you want to persuade them that the advantages of jogging outweigh the disadvantages. If you are speaking on behalf of a company that sells exercise bicycles, you may want them to believe that the cardiovascular benefits of exercise can be accomplished more safely and efficiently with your product than by jogging.

When deciding the specific strategy to use with the pro/con pattern and determining how much time to spend on each side, use the following guidelines:

1. Giving both sides fairly even emphasis is effective when neither side has a clear advantage. You simply want listeners to have all the facts so they can make their own decision. For example, a company offers new employees a choice between two health insurance plans. Current employees are equally split—half favoring one company, half favoring the other.

2. Giving both sides equal emphasis also works well when the weight of evidence is clearly on the side you favor. In other words, you will

be perceived as giving a fair representation of each side, yet after hearing both sides, listeners will make the choice you want them to make.

3. Presenting both sides is most effective when listeners may be initially opposed to your position or side. This way, you in effect disarm listeners by showing them that you understand their current way of thinking.

4. Presenting the favored side first is most effective if the subject is unfamiliar to the listeners, provided you make a strong case for the first side and spend less time and make a less appealing case for the second side. A salesperson once said, "Whoever gets there the *firstest* with the *mostest* gets the sale."

5. Presenting the favored side last may make its acceptance more likely, especially if the other side is shown in a less favorable light. For example, while presenting the least favored side, the speaker is careful to communicate the downside or shortfalls—the weaknesses.

As always, know your audience, organizing with the listeners in mind. Consider the following examples. One outline follows the pro/con plus one strategy; the other uses the staggered strategy.

Pro/Con Pattern—Pro/Con Plus One Strategy

Subject/Title: On-Line Banking

Purpose: To persuade

Objective: TOOTSIFELT decide to bank on-line.

Main Points: I. Advantages of banking on-line

                 II. Disadvantages of banking on-line

                 III. Why the advantages outweigh the disadvantages

---

Pro/Con Pattern—Staggered Strategy

Subject/Title: Bridge at Elk Point

Purpose: To inform

Objective: TOOTSIFELT understand the pros and cons of building a proposed bridge across the river at Elk Point.

Main Points:

        I. Convenience—pros/cons

        II. Cost—pros/cons

        III. Difficulty—pros/cons

TOPICAL

Topically dividing the main points of a talk involves determining categories of the subject. This type of categorizing or classifying often springs directly from the subject itself, which makes it the most common pattern. For instance, a talk about a typical college population might be divided into four points: freshmen, sophomores, juniors, and seniors, with each class division serving as a main point. A speech on university housing might have two points: on-campus housing and off-campus housing. A talk on your three favorite types of music might have the main points of jazz, soft rock, and classical.

At times, the material itself suggests certain strategies for ordering main points. For instance, a talk on the six levels of lesson planning used by many classroom teachers would most likely start with the simplest or lowest level and progressively cover more difficult levels until all six points are covered. More specifically, the first point would be the knowledge level, where the objective is for students to simply recall what was taught. Second would be the comprehension level, where students are expected to go beyond basic recall and to understand or comprehend the relationship of the material to other phenomena. Third would be the application level, where the students are expected to use or apply what is learned to situations in the world around them. Fourth would be the analysis level, where students understand the material so well that they can see the ingredients or parts of the principle, concept, or idea being taught. They can "take it apart" and examine it. Fifth would be the synthesis level, where not only can the students take it apart to analyze it, but they can put the parts together. Sixth would be the evaluation, judgment, expert, or total mastery level. In other words, the talk would follow a simple-to-complex strategy in organizing the treatment of levels at which lessons are taught.

Other talks might follow strategies of known to unknown, general to specific, or specific to general arrangement of points. There are many strategies for arranging points topically. Sometimes, if no compelling order exists, points are treated alphabetically. The important consideration, as with any pattern, is to consider the strategy of arrangement in order to aid your delivery and the listeners' understanding.

The following examples present just three of the many strategies that can be used with the topical pattern of organization. In the first, the speaker wants to inform about the three ways persons receive their officer commissions to enter the Air Force. She decides to take them in the order of which agency is currently commissioning the largest number of Air Force officers.

Topical Pattern—Numbers Strategy (Largest to Smallest)

Subject/Title: Officer Commissioning in the U.S. Air Force

Purpose: To inform

Objective: TOOTSIFELT understand the three ways officers are commissioned.

Main Points:

    I. Officer Training School—commissions the largest number

    II. Air Force Reserve Officer Training Corps

    III. United States Air Force Academy—commissions the fewest

In the next example, the main points are different communication skills. The speaker has chosen to start with the skill that is used most, followed by the second, third, and least-used skill.

Topical Pattern—Most-Used to Least-Used Strategy

Subject/Title: How We Communicate

Purpose: To inform

Objective: TOOTSIFELT comprehend how we use the four basic communication skills.

Main Points:

    I. Listening—50% of the time

    II. Speaking—25% of the time

    III. Reading—15% of the time

    IV. Writing—10% of the time

Speeches to entertain are often arranged topically, often with no apparent strategy except to make the best impact on the audience. The next example is a motivational speech (both entertaining and persuasive) that I have given often.

Topical Pattern—No Apparent Strategy

Subject/Title: The Four E's of Excellent Living

Purpose: To entertain/persuade

Objective: TOOTSIFELT follow the four E's for excellent living.

Main Points:

    I. Enlightenment—learn as much as you can.

    II. Enthusiasm—possess a joy for life.

    III. Encouragement—build up those around you.

    IV. Endurance—never give up.

Notice two things about "The Four E's of Excellent Living." First, I used alliteration. All the points began not only with the same letter but with the same two letters that gave them the same sound. This technique helps listeners remember. It's effective and I use it often. Second, there are 24 different ways to arrange these four main points. Quite frankly, I have tried half of them. But I finally settled on this order for most audiences because it suits them better. They remember the points and are motivated to act.

Most speeches can often be organized in more than one way. Consider the example of the speech "Continents of the World." Notice that the main points are organized alphabetically. They also could be organized geographically—perhaps east to west—or by population, by the time first inhabited, or in a number of different ways. Always organize with your audience in mind.

Topical Pattern—Alphabetical Strategy

Subject/Title: Continents of the World

Purpose: To inform

Objective: TOOTSIFELT know basic facts about the continents.

Main Points:

      I. Africa

     II. Antarctica

    III. Asia

    IV. Australia

     V. Europe

    VI. North America

   VII. South America

Exercise   Recognizing Organizational Patterns

Name the pattern of organization for each set of points. Answers appear on page 44.

1. Subject: Choosing a Sailboat

   Pattern: _topical_
   - Appropriate to the area you'll sail it in
   - Large enough to accommodate the maximum number of people you will carry
   - Condition determined by a licensed boat surveyor

2. Subject: My Experiences Snorkeling

   Pattern: _spatial_
   - In California waters
   - In Bay of Siam
   - In Hawaiian waters

3. Subject: Selecting a Rental Car

   Pattern: _problem & solution_
   - Great variety to choose from
   - Best to rent from a reputable nationwide company

4. Subject: Educational Television

   Pattern: _time_
   - Started in early 1950s
   - Until 1970, emphasis on building more stations
   - Since then, continued program improvement

5. Subject: Getting an Auxiliary Sailboat Under Way

   Pattern: _time_

   - Get sails ready to hoist.
   - Start motor.
   - Cast off.
   - Proceed out of channel.
   - When out of traffic, hoist sails.

6. Subject: States in the Sunbelt

   Pattern: _topical_

   - Alabama
   - Louisiana
   - Florida
   - Georgia
   - Mississippi

7. Subject: How to Prepare to Watch the Big Game on TV

   Pattern: _time_

   - Buy lots of snacks and drinks.
   - Send the kids to the grandparents.
   - Place the remote by your favorite chair.
   - Make it clear that the chair is yours even if you take a break.
   - Strategically locate snacks and drinks near your chair.
   - Turn on the game.

8. Subject: Catching a Cold

   Pattern: _cause & effect_

   - Contact with people and objects in public places
   - Touching eyes, nose, and mouth
   - Sniffles and sneezes

9. Subject: Catching a Cold

   Pattern: _problem/solution_

   - Contact with people and objects in public places
   - Avoid placing hands near eyes, nose, and mouth
   - Stay healthy

10. Subject: Going to Graduate School

Pattern: _____

- Why I should go
- Why I shouldn't go

Exercise   Logical Organization

Tell whether each of the following sets of main points of a speech is organized logically. If not, explain why. Answers appear on page 44.

1. Subject: Selecting a Car   *no*
   - Checking the motor
   - Checking the dealer
   - Checking the body
   - Checking the equipment

2. Subject: Basis for Selecting a Vacation Spot   *yes*
   - Cost
   - Activities
   - Location

3. Subject: Too Much Advertising on Television   *no*
   - The problem of too much advertising on TV is critical.

     Distracting

     Waste of time

     In poor taste
   - The problem could be solved by establishing stricter government controls.

     Could improve content

     Could ensure products are worthwhile

     Could limit the number of commercials per program

4. Subject: Improving High School Teaching of English   *no*
   - More reading assignments are needed
   - Schools in the South where I live are lagging behind
   - Senior classes are not as good as freshman classes

COMBINING PATTERNS

Your talks will make more sense if you use a single pattern to organize main points. You will do a better job presenting, and your audience will listen better.

Hierarchical Consistency

Although you may use a certain organizational pattern for main points, you may use different patterns for subpoints. Still, you will usually attempt to maintain hierarchical consistency. For example, you should attempt to use the same pattern for all sets of subpoints that support main points. And you will most likely be consistent in the pattern you use to arrange points subordinate to subpoints.

Consider the brief *planning outline* in Figure 2.2—called that because it sketches out the basic plan of the presentation—of a talk on Native Tribes in the West. Notice the main points are organized geographically or spatially from south to north (Southwest, Pacific Coast, Northwest). The subpoints of the first main point (Southwest) are organized topically and alphabetically— Apache, Navajo, Pueblo. The three subordinate points under Apache (Early History, Contracts with the Settlers, and Present Conditions) are organized chronologically or by time—using the early-to-late strategy.

Subject/Title: Native Tribes in the West

Purpose: To inform

Objective: TOOTSIFELT know the location of Native tribes in the West.

    I. Southwest

      A. Apache

        1. Early History

        2. Contracts with the Settlers

        3. Present Conditions

      B. Navajo

      C. Pueblo

    II. Pacific Coast

    III. Northwest

FIGURE 2.2 Planning outline.

Most likely, subpoints of the second and third main points (Pacific Coast and Northwest) would also be names of tribes indigenous to the respective regions. They would probably be arranged alphabetically consistent with the subpoints of main point one. Subordinate points under Navajo and Pueblo would most likely be organized chronologically or by time to be consistent with the subordinate points under Apache. No rule says subordinate points must all follow the same organizational structure as those preceding them, but where possible, be consistent. It aids understanding.

Consider the planning outline in Figure 2.3. This planning outline is for a talk on "Nonverbal Communication." The purpose of the talk is to

---

Subject/Title: Nonverbal Communication

Purpose: To inform

Objective: TOOTSIFELT know the importance of nonverbal factors
                  of communication.

I. Internal Factors

  A. Upper Body (head and face)

    1. Positive Effects

    2. Negative Effects

  B. Middle Body (arms, hands, torso)

    1. Positive Effects

    2. Negative Effects

  C. Lower Body (hips, legs, feet)

    1. Positive Effects

    2. Negative Effects

II. External Factors

  A. Objects

    1. Present

    2. Past

  B. Space

    1. Personal

    2. Perceived

  C. Time

FIGURE 2.3   Planning outline.

inform. The objective is for listeners to know the importance of nonverbal factors of communication. Notice that the main points (Internal Factors and External Factors) are arranged topically. The strategy is to start with the more familiar performance factors and then treat the less familiar and often ignored nonperformance factors.

The subpoints for the first main point (Upper Body, Middle Body, and Lower Body) are organized spatially. A pro/con pattern is used to discuss positive and negative effects of each body performance factor. The subpoints of the second main point (Objects, Space, and Time) are organized topically. Again, the strategy is to move from more familiar to less familiar. Research shows people are more conscious of the nonverbal effects of objects and least conscious of time. Subordinate points under IIA (Present and Past) are organized chronologically or by time. Subordinate points under IIB (Personal and Perceived) are organized topically. Point IIC has no subordinate points.

Notice that this speaker's treatment of nonverbal communication will not allow for all subordinate points at a given level to follow the same organizational structure. Still, the plan does show consistency for points subordinate to a given point.

Remember: Each set of main points and subordinate points should follow a logical pattern of organization.

Outlining

You've seen examples of two planning outlines—one on "Native Tribes in the West," the other on "Nonverbal Communication." Chapter 8 discusses *preparation outlines*—those that include all the points, supporting material, the beginning, the ending, and connectors or transitions that tie the material together. In short, the preparation outline contains everything about the talk. It enables you to come back to your talk and give it at a later time. Chapter 8 also discusses a third kind of outline, the *presentation outline*. This is the outline you'll use when you actually present the briefing, lecture, or speech. It will be shorter than the preparation outline but will contain more material than the planning outline.

At this point, however, you only need to be concerned with the planning outline. As you plan your talk, make a tentative outline—a planning outline—similar to ones used in the examples in this chapter. Keep your listeners in mind as you prepare this brief outline. The organization patterns and strategies you choose at this time will provide structure to the body of your talks. However, know that quite often even experienced speakers revise outlines three or four times before being satisfied and finally putting them into final form for the talk. Sometimes this revision occurs as the speakers choose supporting material for the points they plan to make.

Standard Outline Format

A standard outline format lets you see the relationships among main points, subordinate points, and supporting material in the talk. The previous examples have followed the standard format of using Roman numerals for main points, capital letters for subpoints, and Arabic numerals for points subordinate to the subpoints. Lowercase letters are generally used for the next level of subordinate points. You will seldom, if ever, subdivide beyond this level. If you do, you may enclose numbers or letters in parentheses to distinguish them from higher-order points. Indentation serves to further clarify the different hierarchy or level of points.

    I. First main point
       A. First subpoint of main point I
       B. Second subpoint of main point I
          1. First point subordinate to IB
          2. Second point subordinate to IB
             a. First point subordinate to IB2
             b. Second point subordinate to IB2
                (1.) First point subordinate to IB2b
                (2.) Second point subordinate to IB2b
                    (a.) First point subordinate to IB2b(2)
                    (b.) Second point subordinate to IB2b(2)

Note: Continue this method for succeeding main points. Also, at any time there may be more than two points or subpoints. I used two here to show one method of lettering and numbering points. Also, if a point takes more than one line, then succeeding lines begin directly under the first word of the preceding line.

The organization patterns and strategies you choose provide the basis for the planning outline and therefore provide structure to the body of your presentation. But structure without content is not enough. You also need interesting and effective supporting material. I have listened to some pretty good talks that were not organized as well as they could have been or should have been. Still, I enjoyed them and learned from them. But I seldom have enjoyed or remembered material well when the speech did not contain good and appropriate supporting material. Supporting material defines the talk and holds listener interest. To use an anatomical analogy, the organization provides the skeleton and the supporting material supplies the flesh. Whether talking about cars, houses, people, or speeches, it's what's on the frame that attracts us and holds our interest.

> *Organization is the skeleton for the body; supporting material is the flesh. The right flesh makes the body attractive and appealing.* **INSIGHT**

The next four chapters tell how to put flesh on the skeleton. Chapter 3 focuses on clarification support—definitions, comparisons and contrasts, and examples. Chapter 4 treats proof support—testimony, and statistics. Chapter 5 focuses on using humorous support. Chapter 6 tells how to use visual support.

Check Yourself: What Have You Learned?

☐ Clear organization is vital to effective speaking.

☐ Organization must fit the subject, purpose, and objective of the talk.

☐ Above all, organization must meet the needs of the listeners.

☐ Different strategies can be used with each of the six major patterns of organization.

☐ A time pattern is a natural way of arranging sequential events.

☐ A spatial pattern describes relationships according to some direction.

☐ A causal pattern shows how one set of conditions causes another.

☐ The problem/solution pattern presents a problem and then proposes a way to solve it.

☐ The pro/con talk pattern treats both sides of an issue but may favor one side.

☐ The topical pattern divides points of a talk into categories of the subject.

☐ Different patterns may be used in a talk—one for main points; others for subordinate ones.

☐ Attempt to maintain hierarchical consistency when organizing a talk—that is, use the same pattern for all sets of subordinate points that support main points.

☐ Use a standard outline format to see the relationships among main points, subordinate points, and supporting material in the talk.

☐ The planning outline precedes the preparation outline and the presentation outline.

ANSWERS

Recognizing Organizational Patterns

1. Topical
2. Space
3. Problem/Solution
4. Time
5. Time
6. Topical
7. Time
8. Cause/Effect
9. Problem/Solution
10. Pro/Con

Logical Organization

1. No. Not equivalent points—first two and last are concerned with car itself; the second is not.
2. Yes.
3. No. The solutions presented do not solve the problem.
4. No. Not consistent. The first point is a topical point, the second is space, and the third is either time or topical (depending on what the speaker emphasizes).

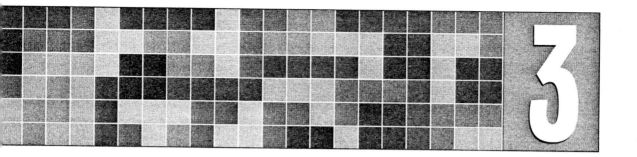

Using Clarification Support

OBJECTIVE

- To comprehend how to use clarification support in a presentation

TASKS

- Discuss the types of definitions, and give guidelines for using them.
- Discuss the types of examples, and give guidelines for using them.
- Discuss the types of comparisons, and give guidelines for using them.

Why are some people easier to listen to than others? Why are their presentations more enjoyable? Why can you remember more of what they say? There are many reasons. The subject of the talk, the way it's organized and adapted to you as an audience member, and the speaker's style and method of delivery are factors. But another thing that often sets apart a good presentation from a poor one is its use of engaging supporting materials to back up ideas and main points. Many "ho hum" talks could be very good with effective supporting materials. Good supporting materials hold the listeners' attention; substantiate a claim or position the speaker wants listeners to accept; and help listeners understand, remember, and believe what is said.

Let's face it—listeners find it difficult to understand or accept unsupported ideas or assertions. Suppose, for instance, you are giving a speech on "How to Organize a Talk." You say, "Talks can be organized according to one of several patterns of presentation. The most common are time, space, cause/effect, problem/solution, pro/con, and topical." Most likely, you will need to supply more information if your listeners are actually to use these patterns in their own writing or speaking. You'll need to explain each pattern as I did in Chapter 2. Not only did I explain them, but I gave examples of each. Those examples were my supporting material.

Listeners may have trouble remembering main points, sometimes even when the presentation is well organized and on a subject that interests them. But give a definition that focuses audience attention, use an interesting example, draw a memorable comparison, give a startling statistic, use an arresting quotation, or tell a humorous anecdote, and the audience remembers it. Support may be verbal—the words we use—or it may be visual—the pictures we see (charts, graphs, PowerPoint slides, even the personal image speakers project and the nonverbal behavior they demonstrate).

Support material—that is, material used to clarify, prove, or in some way illustrate a point—is so important that this chapter and the following three chapters address how to use it effectively. This chapter focuses on clarification support; chapter 4, on proof support; chapter 5, on humorous support; and chapter 6, on visual support. This, the longest of the four chapters, focuses on the three kinds of verbal clarification support—definitions, examples, and comparisons.

DEFINITIONS

"What do you mean by that?" is a frequent and necessary question in conversation. Unfortunately, listeners can't ask this question during speeches. Therefore, you as a speaker need to anticipate the question and answer it for them. Define words that may be misunderstood or words that you may use in a special way.

To establish a common ground of understanding, define abstract or confusing words early in the presentation. At times, when a term is going to appear throughout the talk, you will define it in the introduction. If you are trying to communicate an idea, you'll often need to explain exactly what you are talking about. Clear up any possible misunderstanding concerning the meaning of any word, phrase, or concept that might seem confusing, vague, or irrelevant to your audience. Semanticists—people who study words and their meanings—point out: "Meanings are not in words; meanings are in people." Or, "Words have no meaning; people have meanings." That is, the meaning of a word exists in the mind of the user, not in the word itself or in the object it represents. Speakers communicate effectively insofar as they and their audiences attach similar meanings to the words used. It's up to the speaker to make certain the audience attaches the intended meaning to words used in the speech, lecture, or briefing.

"'When I use a word,' Humpty Dumpty said, in a rather scornful tone, 'it means just what I choose it to mean—neither more nor less.'"

—Lewis Carroll, *Alice's Adventures in Wonderland*

Why Definitions Are Important

Why do audiences need definitions? Another way to ask the question is: why do we have so many misunderstandings that center around the meanings of words? There are several explanations:

1. *Sometimes words sound like other words.* Recently a speaker was describing the advantages of a new digital television service available to viewers. He said the new service had three advantages over other plans: "First, the picture is clearer. Second, more channels are available. Third, and perhaps most important, is the popular 'paper view.' " For several minutes, the speaker talked about this "paper view." Only gradually did the listeners realize he was not saying "paper view" but "pay per view."

Misunderstanding could have been avoided if the first time the speaker used the term he had said something like this: "The new service also offers the opportunity for you to watch recent movies from the comfort of your own home by paying each time you choose to view one of them. This 'pay per view' feature—that is, paying each time you view one of these movies—has been very popular with subscribers in other places."

It's not how the word sounds; it's what associations it stimulates that counts.

—Dr. James Vickrey, noted speaker and professor of Speech Communication, Troy State University, Alabama

2. *Sometimes the words are new.* With increasing specialization and rapid advances in technology, the development of new words or terms races ahead of dictionaries and common usage. For example, the exploding popularity of home computers has introduced us to new terminology. Several years ago, someone asked me how much RAM I had. I didn't have

a clue what the person was talking about. I felt sure he was not asking me about a male sheep, or a plunger in a force pump, or a battering ram on the front of a ship. I asked for clarification. The person said, "You know RAM—random access memory—on your computer." I needed still more definition for clarification. After much questioning, I learned RAM is computer memory that contains special-purpose information (like a program) that can't be altered. That helped, but I kept asking questions. Finally, I thought I understood. Then the other person said, "Don't confuse RAM with ROM—read only memory." I would have been better off without the last statement. He gave me too much information. Now I was confused again.

3. *Words often have more than one meaning.* A speaker says, "I'll only talk about 5 minutes." To me, 5 minutes means just that, 5 minutes—300 seconds. To him, "5 minutes" means anywhere from 5 to 15 minutes. Or, I tell my colleague that the temperature in the office is quite comfortable. My "quite comfortable," however, is her "uncomfortable." For me, 76 degrees is comfortable; for her, 70 degrees is comfortable. The same word can mean different things to different people.

In another example, a doctor put an overweight patient on a diet. "Eat regularly for two days, then skip a day," he said. "Follow this pattern for a month, and then come back and see me. After a month you should lose 10 pounds." A month later, the man came back for his appointment. He had lost twenty pounds. The doctor was delighted. He said, "You lost all that weight just by following my instructions?" "Yes," said the patient, "but I thought I was going to drop dead on that third day." "From hunger?" "No," said the man, "from skipping." This cute story reminds us that the same words can mean different things to different people.

INSIGHT	*Words do have more than one meaning: the sign said, "Fine for Parking Here," and since it was fine, I parked there.*

4. *Different words can mean the same things.* A teacher asked students to come to the next class ready to relate an anecdote from their personal experience. After class, a student asked if she could just tell a short, interesting story instead. The teacher told her that's what an anecdote is—a short, interesting story. Different words can mean the same thing. From that day on, the teacher never made that assignment without first defining or telling what an anecdote is.

In the midwestern United States, people drink "pop." In the South, people often call it a "cold drink," "soft drink," "cola," and even "coke"—though it may not even be a Coca-Cola. In other places, it's called a "soda."

Most midwesterners would never call it a soda, because to them a soda is something with ice cream in it. In Boston, the midwesterner's soda is called a "frappe." And interestingly, just a few miles away in Newport, Rhode Island, the same drink is called a "cabinet." Different words can have the same meaning. Failing to acknowledge that multiple words can share the same meaning often leads to miscommunication.

5. *Some words have strong emotional meanings that block or overshadow the intended meaning.*   Consider the word *failure.* The word often has a negative meaning or connotation—we fail a test, fail to get selected for a job, or experience a failed relationship. Such failure produces a negative emotional reaction in us. As failures mount, we begin to fear failure. Perhaps even the mention of the word *failure* affects us emotionally. Yet, failure may be good. A test fails to show the presence of cancer cells. A bomb planted in a public place fails to detonate, thereby sparing human life. Speakers must be careful to define words that may have unintended meanings for their listeners.

For example, while assigning students to prepare and present a five-minute informative speech, the teacher says students will receive criticism both from the teacher and from other students. For most people, criticism has a negative meaning, so the teacher goes on to define criticism as he is using it. "By *criticism,* I don't mean just pointing out the weaknesses or problems in the organization, support, and delivery of the speeches. Rather, I use the word *criticism* to include the strengths of both preparation and presentation of these speeches. We learn by criticism that uncovers both the strengths and the weaknesses. As critics of one anothers' speeches, we will do our best job analyzing the speech and the performance of the speaker so we can all learn."

6. *The meanings of words change over time.*   At one time, the word *access* meant something that you had or didn't have—as in having access to a building or to information. Today, everybody seems to need access. Lack of access must be corrected. One view is that all people should have access to higher education; otherwise, they will have been "denied access." Certainly, disabled persons must have access to buildings, and we need access to public records. Before we finish discussing the word *access,* note that people now want to be able to access computer files by phone. The word *access* has acquired new meaning. Appearance of *access* as a transitive verb—as in accessing one's records—is fairly recent.

The point is clear. Language and word use change over time. If you don't think this is so, study documents that are 100 years old. For more of a challenge, read English literature that is 200, 400, or 600 years old. Furthermore, language and word meaning is changing now more than ever before. Speakers must account for this change and, when necessary, define words carefully for listeners.

INSIGHT   *Constant change is here to stay.*

Exercise   Word Meanings

1. Choose a word—such as *cut, dog, draw, end, fair, fast, give, hand, heavy, jump, mad, name, open, pass,* or *quarter*—that has many meanings. Write a 250-word essay or give a two-minute speech in which you use that word at least 10 different ways. You may use a dictionary.

2. For a greater challenge, do the same exercise again, this time using five common words in the same essay or speech each in five different ways.

Types of Definitions

Definitions may range in length from one word to an entire speech. They may define words, phrases, or acronyms. Sometimes definition is by classi-fication—putting the term into a general class to which it belongs and then differentiating it from other members in the class. At other times, opera-tional definitions are given—explaining how a word or phrase works or what it does. The purpose and objective of the speech and the knowledge of the audience affect how a speaker uses definitions as support.

Short Definitions

Sometimes a one- or two-word definition will be enough to clarify the meaning of an unfamiliar word to the audience. For example, *disseminate* can be easily defined as "spread widely." A speaker wouldn't say, "The word *disseminate* means to spread widely." This comes across as "talking down" to the audience. Instead, she might say, "We want to make certain to dissemi-nate this information. We need to spread it widely."

In another example, a teacher said to her class, "One of the most salient points to remember for this test . . . " Then she paused briefly and thought, "The word *salient* is not familiar to my listeners." So she continued, "One of the most important, prominent things to keep is mind is . . ." Notice what she did. She didn't say, "I think I used a word you didn't know," or "By *salient,* I mean prominent or important." Instead, she used synonyms in a follow-on sentence that simply clarified what she'd said rather than "talking down" to her audience. Speakers are responsible for clearly and appropri-ately defining words the audience may not understand.

At times, speakers must define words that are often loosely employed. As stated earlier, some words simply have different meanings for different people. Words such as *democracy, equal rights, security needs,* and *loyalty* can usually be defined easily. Sometimes a speaker may seek novel and memorable ways to define such terms. *Pragmatism* might be defined as "a fancy word that means the proof of the pudding is in the eating." It's the speaker's responsibility to understand the audience's knowledge level and then match definitions to what they need to know in a way that helps them understand and remember.

Extended Definitions

At times, definitions must be longer. In a speech about farms in the Midwest, a speaker mentions a "quarter section." He then defines a section as a piece of land a mile on each of its four sides and says a section of land is often divided into quarters—four farms half a mile on each side. A quarter section, then, is the size of many farms. In another example, a former prisoner of war was defining what the word *sacrifice* means: "When you see an American prisoner giving up his meager ration of fish just so another American who is sick can have a little more to eat, that is sacrifice. Because when you don't have anything, and you give it up, or you have very little and you give it up, then you're hurting yourself, and that is true sacrifice. That's what I saw in the prison camp."

An entire talk may be needed to define and introduce listeners to a subject. For example, when introducing a new process or way of doing things, an entire lecture or briefing might consist of defining the process or procedure. A teacher lecturing on the concept of "transactional communication" might spend the entire lecture defining and explaining that the transactional approach means to consider the total communication process and the interaction of the various parts of the process on one another. Other forms of support material, such as examples and comparisons, would be needed to fully define what was meant. Definitions vary in length depending on the subject, purpose, and objective of the speech and, above all, on the needs of the listeners.

Definitions of Acronyms

Acronyms are words formed from the initial letter or letters of each of the successive parts or major parts of a compound term (such as NATO—North Atlantic Treaty Organization; RADAR—radio detecting and ranging; and SNAFU—situation normal all fouled up). Perhaps giving the actual words themselves, as in the preceding sentence, would be enough, but sometimes more information is needed. With NATO, the audience may need to be reminded of the member nations and partner countries. Perhaps a speaker would also state NATO's major purpose or mission or tell of recent developments. RADAR, on the other hand, is a common term. You would not need to define it or even tell what the letters stand for. Depending on the audience, you may or may not have to define SNAFU, although you might mention that the term originated during World War II when soldiers used it to describe a chaotic and confused situation.

Consider a talk on PME—professional military education. The audience needs to know what the letters *PME* stand for since a quick Internet search reveals over 25 different meanings for PME, including pattern matching engine, parity modulating encoder, and product management engineer. But most audiences would need more than a simple identification of PME as professional military education. The speaker would need to explain that PME consists of a series of courses to be taken throughout their careers by officers and enlisted personnel from all branches of the U.S. military—Army, Navy, Air Force, and Marines. Then, depending on the speaker's objective and the kind of audience, PME might need to be defined in more detail.

Suppose a speaker talks about students taking the ACT and doesn't explain what the letters *ACT* stand for. Listeners might think a person is going to be in a play. Or if listeners know ACT is a test, they might believe it is some sort of an act or action test—perhaps something that measures a motor performance skill. The speaker would need to explain that ACT stands for American College Testing program and then further explain that the results of the test predict a student's ability to perform well in future academic situations.

Definitions by Classification

Dictionaries often define by classification—that is, the word is placed in a general class or group and then is differentiated from other members of its class. You can do this without a dictionary, but quoting from a reputable dictionary adds credibility to your definition. Consider the following examples of definition by classification from *Merriam-Webster's Collegiate Dictionary*.

- *Angus:* "any of a breed of usually black hornless beef cattle originating in Scotland." Note that *Angus* is placed in a larger class—cattle—and then differentiated from other members of the class by being black, hornless, and originating in Scotland. Other cattle may share some characteristics, but if they have all three, then by definition they are Angus cattle.
- *Quonset:* "a prefabricated shelter set on a foundation of bolted steel trusses and built of a semicircular arching roof of corrugated metal insulated with wood fiber." *Quonset* is part of a larger class—shelters. Other shelters may be prefabricated or have bolted steel trusses, but only a Quonset possesses all of the attributes or characteristics in the definition.

- *Pickup:* "a light truck having an enclosed cab and an open body with low sides and tailgate." *Pickup* belongs to a larger class—trucks— but only the pickup truck has all of the characteristics given in the definition.

Defining by classification offers the advantage of following the format of most good speaking and writing, which starts with the general situation and then focuses on the specific situation—much like pouring liquid into a funnel so it moves to a focal point or into a conduit or central channel.

Operational Definitions

Sometimes a word or phrase may be familiar to the audience, but the speaker chooses to use it in a specific or unusual way, usually in a way that is precise, measurable, and concrete. For example, a speaker reports on an experimental study on the results of using different kinds of evidential support material in six short speeches. He varies the level of evidence so that for each speech three versions were prepared: one with "specific evidence," one with "nonspecific evidence," and one with what he termed "no evidence." He tells how he operationally defined these three levels of evidence in his study: "I defined specific evidence as where the speeches contained specific statistics, dates, and places. With nonspecific evidence, messages contained less specific information, characterized by such terms as *many, most,* and *probably.* Messages with no evidence were those where the evidence in the message was deleted or replaced by such things as 'probably more,' and sentences were often prefaced by 'It,' 'It seems,' 'It appears,' and so forth." Since evidence can be defined in different ways, the speaker tells the definition he used in his study.

In a speech on "Dealing with the Disabled," the speaker may say, "By *disabled* I mean any person having a physical or mental impairment that substantially limits one or more major life activities." A speech on the welfare of children might operationally define abuse and neglect as "the physical and mental injury, sexual abuse, negligent treatment, or maltreatment of a child under age 18 by another person."

Operational definitions are usually not found in dictionaries. Rather, they are original and are created to communicate the speaker's exact meaning to the audience.

Guidelines for Using Definitions

Following certain guidelines will ensure that you use definitions effectively— in a way that gets the desired results.

1. *Don't overuse definitions.* Recently, a motivational speaker began by saying, "I want to tell you how to be a motivator. The dictionary defines

motivator as 'one who motivates' or 'provides a motive.' " This definition was unnecessary and boring, and it insulted the intelligence of the audience. At this point, they began to lose their motivation to listen to him. A few moments later, it got worse when he said, "The first thing a motivator must be is an encourager. The dictionary defines *encourager* as 'one who inspires with courage, spirit, or hope.' " Don't use definitions unless the term is relatively obscure or has several possible definitions.

Overusing definitions will tax the memory of listeners. One or two definitions are difficult for listeners to remember; several may be impossible. If presenting several definitions is crucial to the talk, then consider posting them where the audience can see them or distribute a handout to each listener with the definitions printed out for easy reference. At the very least, project them via PowerPoint or some other method while you recite them. Most people will benefit from seeing as well as hearing the definitions.

2. *Use generally accepted definitions.*   Even operational definitions should be similar to those found in a dictionary. For example, you wouldn't say, "For purposes of this talk, *extroversion* will be defined as 'a tendency to be shy and withdrawn.' " This would be confusing. Remember the first time you heard somebody say something like, "That's a *bad* car." It probably took a while to realize *bad* meant "good." A speech is not the place to introduce a new definition, especially one that doesn't align with generally accepted ones.

3. *Don't use a defined term to mean something else later on.*   A speaker defines the term *drug* as "any chemical substance, whether of natural or synthetic origin, that can be used to alter perception, mood, or other psychological states." Later on, the speaker uses *drug* to refer to a medicine that reduces inflammation from arthritis. This reference confuses listeners since the speaker's operational definition of *drug* did not cover any medicinal drugs used to treat physical ailments. Once a term is defined, the speaker should try to avoid using the word in a different context in the same speech.

4. *Define terms with your audience in mind.*   The perspective of listeners varies with their experience. For example, the chief financial officer (CFO) and staff of a company would most likely not have the background to understand technical definitions given by a computer technician, whereas the chief information officer (CIO) and staff would. By the same token, the CFO would understand accounting terminology and definitions, whereas the CIO might not. Definitions must suit the audience.

5. *Don't define a word, term, or concept with one equally difficult to understand.*   A speaker says, "The subject is very *recondite*." An audience member asks, "What do you mean by *recondite*?" The speaker replies, "Esoteric, hermetic, you know, recondite." The speaker probably should have used the word *deep* or *difficult* in the first place. Certainly, either would have been a better word than *esoteric* or *hermetic* to define *recondite*.

Definitions are often indispensable supporting material. They provide a common ground for understanding when terms may have more than one meaning or when the audience may not attach the speaker's intended meaning to a word or phrase. Of course, not all presentations will need definitions. However, the same thing cannot be said for examples. Most speeches benefit from the use of sound examples, which make an abstract or difficult-to-understand idea easier to understand.

Exercise   Defining Terms

1. Think of an everyday appliance, such as a dishwasher, clothes dryer, iron, refrigerator, or stove. Pretend that you have just met someone from a foreign country who has never heard of the item. Define that item for the person.

2. Pick some item from your desk, your room, or your office. How would you describe and define that item to a contemporary? To someone from a different generation? Different culture? Would you define the item differently for different people? Why or why not?

3. Select a term that is specific to your job field or area of study. How would you clarify its meaning to someone from outside your field or area of study?

EXAMPLES

In the course of conversation, people will often say something like "Give me an example of what you are talking about," or they will ask questions for clarification. If audiences were permitted to stop speakers, they would say the same things. Speakers bear the responsibility of anticipating such questions and answering them by giving examples to clarify the points they are making.

Types of Examples

Examples are usually classified as short or long, real or invented. While these classifications help us to understand their use, all examples have this in common: they clarify; they help listeners understand. They make an abstract or difficult idea concrete or easy to grasp.

Short examples or instances.   Speakers give instances to briefly and clearly support a point. If the instance allows listeners to grasp the idea or concept immediately, then it has done its job. Suppose a speaker wants to make the point that older adults should not give up, that perseverance pays. He might use this short example or instance to reinforce or support his point: "At age sixty-five, Harlan had lost all his money. His only income was his paltry Social Security check. Many people would have given up, but not Harlan. He knew how to fry chicken, and within a few years Colonel Harlan Sanders and his Kentucky Fried Chicken business was worth millions."

Long examples or illustrations.   They amplify, clarify and explain a point in detail by supplying narrative, descriptive details. An example becomes a story or a sketch of the circumstances. Whereas the instance or short example might be given in 10 seconds or less, the longer example or illustration might take up to several minutes. Consider how the Sanders instance might be developed into a longer illustration:

> "Several years ago, a man in his early sixties was offered nearly $200,000 for a restaurant/motel/service station business that he had spent his life building up. He refused the offer because he loved his business and just wasn't ready to retire yet. Then the state built a new highway bypassing his business, and he lost it. He was flat broke. His only income was a paltry Social Security check. Most people in that condition at age sixty-five would have been crushed. They would have lived out their lives, just hanging on, trying to make it from month to month—Social Security check to Social Security check— but not Harlan. He wasn't ready to quit. He would avoid the pitfall that traps so many people over age 60. He would not fall into the way of thinking that it's too late to do anything. After all, there was one thing he knew. He knew how to fry chicken. He knew it well! Maybe he could sell that knowledge to others. He kissed his wife good-bye, and in a battered old car, with a pressure cooker and a can of specially prepared flour, set out to sell his idea to other restaurants. It was tough going, and he often slept in the car because he didn't have enough money for a hotel room. But he persevered. And a few years later, Colonel Harlan Sanders had built a nationwide franchised restaurant chain called Kentucky Fried Chicken."

The illustration or longer example gives listeners time to digest and appreciate the point. An appropriate illustration used well helps listeners remember the point, sometimes long after the speech is over. It could be that every time they drive by a Kentucky Fried Chicken establishment, their thoughts will be drawn to the story of the older adult who persevered.

Examples are not only long or short; they also can be real or invented. Each type has its advantages. Each will help listeners understand a point the speaker is trying to make.

Real examples.   Speakers might use real examples of things that happened to other people. The Colonel Sanders example is a real example. It actually happened. Sometimes speakers' most effective real examples come from their own experience. Often, when speaking about communication, I make the point mentioned earlier in this chapter that "the same words can mean different things to different people." I illustrate the point as follows:

> "Some years ago, when I was a professor of speech communication at the University of Missouri in Columbia, I called my wife and asked her to pick me up at the circle drive near Switzler Hall, where my office was located. I wasn't thinking very clearly, for there were two circle drives. One was a handy little circle that came right up to the back door. The other was a larger, more impressive drive that came within 50 yards of the front door. People often drove up the front drive to get a scenic view of the old red brick campus. Well, you guessed it. I went to the smaller, less impressive drive. My wife went to the larger one. At about the same time, we both figured out what had happened. I came around to the front of the building just in time to see her pull away. Even then I didn't guess where she was headed. After a few trips back and forth, we finally got together. Since then, when things aren't clear, one of us asks, 'Just which circle drive are you talking about?' The same words can mean different things to different people."

Invented examples.   The invented example—sometimes called the constructed, fictitious, or hypothetical example—is just what its name implies. Speakers either use examples someone else invented or draw on their own imagination and judgment to make up examples that support the points they want to make. A speaker told the following story to make the point that things won't change unless attitudes change:

> "Little 10-year old Freddy woke up in a bad mood. At breakfast, he took one bite of his pancakes and said, 'Yucky! This is the worst stuff I've ever tasted.' Freddy's mother told him to go back upstairs and come back in a better mood. She added, 'We'll just pretend this never happened.' In a few minutes, Freddy was back downstairs. He sat in the same chair and grumbled, 'Humph, looks like somebody took a bite out of my pancakes.'"

We all encounter situations where we need to start over and pretend nothing has happened. But unless we change our attitude, what we pretend did not happen will probably happen again. The pancakes won't improve until we do.

The story of Freddy could be true, but most likely it was invented—made up by either the speaker or someone else. Whatever the case, it effectively supports the point. When using invented examples, keep a couple of things in mind. First, do not start by saying, "This actually happened." The story is just as effective without it. Also, such a claim hurts your credibility, for people in the audience may know the story is invented, especially if they've heard it before. Second, do not claim the story happened to you if it didn't. I've been in an audience when someone told the circle drive story related earlier as if it actually happened to him. The audience had heard me tell the story, so they concluded the speaker was lying. Claiming something happened to you when it hasn't demonstrates ethical irresponsibility and harms your credibility. An exception to this point can be made when speakers are obviously using a story to make themselves or others the object of humor, a point we will discuss again in Chapter 5.

Guidelines for Using Examples

Whether your examples are instances or illustrations, real or invented, eight considerations are important when choosing examples. Each can be summarized with one word.

Representative.   Examples should accurately represent the points they support. At times, speakers are guilty of misrepresentation. For instance, a salesperson complaining about customers gives examples of three problem people she has dealt with recently and passes them off as typical. The truth is, they were unusual; they were in the minority and didn't represent all the people she had dealt with. Or, a man marketing apples places a dozen of the nicest ones on the table and claims these represent the produce he has available. The truth is these are the best he has to offer; the others are not as good. A speaker claims to be an expert on investing and gives two examples of exceptionally shrewd advice that allowed his clients to make money, but he fails to describe the times he lost much money for his clients. If the salesperson had informed the audience these were examples of the worst customers, or if the man had said the displayed apples were his best, or if the financial advisor had said these were examples of some of the best advice he had given, then these three speakers would be justified in using the examples they chose. But if examples are purported to *represent* something, then they must be typical.

Clear.   Examples should clarify or shed light on the point, not confuse the listeners. A 50-year-old speaker addressing a group of college students says, "Remember when we watched the Vietnam War from our living rooms." The typical college students don't remember, since they weren't born yet. An engineer talking to a group of farmers launches into a highly technical example to illustrate a new agricultural engineering development, which the farmers don't understand. Make sure your examples clarify the point you are making and do not confuse your listeners.

Relevant.   Speakers are often tempted to use interesting, humorous, or easy-to-relate examples even if they lack relevancy to the subject or point they are trying to make. Perhaps they've told a story before and know it gets a good response from the audience. But if the story doesn't fit, then don't use it. A speaker making the point that people do stupid things used this example:

> "Six seamen were bedding down in hammocks for their first night at sea in a cabin. For hours, they tossed and turned in the stuffy cabin, unable to sleep. Finally, one seaman got out of his hammock and went to the porthole. 'I know we're not supposed to do this,' he said, 'but I am going to open the porthole'; the others agreed it was a good idea. When he cranked open the porthole, they all breathed easier and slept like babies the rest of the night. In the morning, when they went to close the porthole, they saw that it was sealed with an outer glass pane and that no fresh air had entered the cabin that night."

This would be an outstanding story if the speaker were making the point that our perception determines reality for us—in other words, that what we believe influences how we feel. As he told the story to illustrate that people do stupid things, however, I thought maybe he was going to say the seamen were in a submarine. Then opening a window would be stupid. As the speaker went to his next point, I was telling myself that perhaps the seamen were disobedient, but they weren't stupid. Make sure your examples are relevant.

Appropriate. Know your audience. A story that might be appropriate to motivate a group of elite Army Rangers ready to go on a mission might be inappropriate for a high school class. Although you can adjust and use different examples for different audiences, one very good rule to follow is this: *never use any story—instance or illustration, real or invented—that you wouldn't want the world to know that you used.* Ask yourself this question: Would I want my grandmother, mother, wife, husband, child, priest, minister, or rabbi—or person of a different ethnic or racial origin—to know that I used this example? If not, don't use it.

Of course, an example might be suited to the audience but not appropriate for a given occasion. For example, humor may be inappropriate for a solemn occasion. It's impossible to state all the rules for good sense and tact in choosing examples, but it's always better to err on the side of caution. If you are not sure whether to use a particular example, don't.

Interesting. Examples must hold audience interest. Representative, clear, relevant, appropriate ones may still be dull. When the speech gets dull, interest wanes. One value of interesting examples is they reclaim or retain the interest of the audience. In this chapter, I have attempted to use interesting examples. If the supporting material isn't interesting and engaging, you'll lose your audience. So think about your audience, and know what interests them.

Personalized. One way to interest the audience is to personalize your examples. Real examples have the advantage of having actually happened. If they happened to you, their personal nature helps you to draw a word picture audiences can visualize. That's why the circle drive story has such appeal. I tell it on myself, it actually happened in a specific place, and it's clear how miscommunication occurs. The story communicates these things clearly. But examples that happened to other people can also be personalized for the audience. Supply names, places, times, and other details so audience members can visualize and understand the example. Invented examples can also benefit from being personalized or placed in context. Consider the following example a speaker invented to illustrate priorities. He introduces the example by saying, "It's important to take care of first things first."

> "A farm boy accidentally overturned his wagonload of corn. A neighboring farmer heard the noise. 'Hey, Billy!' the farmer yelled. 'Don't worry about it. Come on over and eat dinner with us; then after we eat I'll help you get the wagon up.' 'That's mighty nice of you,' Billy answered, 'but I don't think Pa would like me to.' 'Aw, come on,' the farmer insisted. 'Well, okay,' the boy finally agreed and added, 'but Pa won't like it.' After a hearty dinner, Billy thanked his host. 'I feel a lot better now, but I know Pa is going to be real upset.' 'Don't be foolish,' the neighbor said with a smile. 'By the way, where is he?' 'Under the wagon,' replied Billy."

Then the speaker goes on to say, "Billy knew what was most important, but he failed to put first things first."

Consider how much more effective this story is in holding the audience's attention and helping them visualize the situation than if the speaker had not given details—a farm boy, a wagonload of corn, a neighboring farmer, the dialogue of each speaker, and so forth. What if the speaker had just said, "A man persuaded a neighbor boy to come eat dinner with him even though the boy protested that his father wouldn't like it if he didn't get his overturned wagon right side up first. But the boy went to dinner with the man. After dinner, the man asked the boy where his father was, and the boy told the man he was under the wagon." It just doesn't have the same impact, does it? Personalize your examples for the greatest effect.

Short.   Lengthy examples are sometimes effective, especially in long talks. A 45-minute talk may have several lengthy illustrations, perhaps each 2 or 3 minutes long. But a 2- or 3-minute illustration is most likely out of place in a 5- or 10-minute speech. Exceptions may exist, but too much time devoted to one or two long, illustrative examples often robs content from the speech. While a well-placed and well-told illustration may make a point, the speaker should make the point in the speech and then use instances, illustrations, and other supporting material to "bring the point home," or support the idea or point made.

Clustered.   Often, short examples or instances can be clustered together to help listeners gain a more complete understanding of a point. For example, a speaker identifies spoonerisms as one barrier to effective communication. He explains that spoonerisms are a transposition of the initial sounds of two or more words and are named after British clergyman and educator William Archibald Spooner—a nervous man whose tongue frequently got tangled up when he spoke. The speaker goes on to cluster examples of spoonerisms to help his audience understand: "Is the bean dizzy?" ("Is the dean busy?"); "I'll have a coff of cuppee" ("I'll have a cup of coffee"); "A half-warmed fish within us" ("A half-formed wish within us"); "I'd like to have a chilled greese" ("I'd like to have a grilled cheese").

Earlier we read how a speaker used an example of the perseverance of Colonel Harlan Sanders to show that older adults should not give up. Suppose the speaker wants to support the point that people who persevere accomplish great things. Rather than use a single illustration, he might cluster several instances:

> "Edison didn't give up on the lightbulb even though his helpers seriously doubted it would ever work; Michelangelo kept pounding and painting regardless of put-downs; Lindbergh ignored the doubts of others and flew nonstop across the Atlantic; and General Douglas MacArthur promised during the darkest days of World War II, 'I shall return.' History is replete with examples of people who succeeded because they persevered."

Whatever kind of examples you use—short or long, real or invented—the guidelines given above will help you as you decide which examples to use in a presentation.

Exercise   Using Examples

1. Tell about one of your best friends. Use examples to help your listeners understand why this person is such a good friend—perhaps an instance of how she came to your aid or perhaps a clustering of such instances. Perhaps you will want to use a longer illustration that shows just what a good friend this person is.

2. Use examples to support one of the following assertions:

    The stock market is the best (or worst) place to invest.

    A college education is necessary (or not necessary) for success.

    People skills are more important than work skills for getting ahead in a company (or vice versa).

COMPARISONS

Comparisons support a point the speaker is making by demonstrating its similarity to another idea, object, or situation. Comparisons, then, along with definitions and examples, can provide outstanding explanation and clarification for a statement the speaker wants to support. Sometimes an unknown or little understood item is placed beside a similar but better-known item. At other times, a difficult idea is made clear by comparing it with a simpler one. At still other times, speakers draw comparisons between dissimilar items to contrast or show differences. In any case, comparisons are an important means of verbal support.

Types of Comparisons

Speakers use four types of comparisons—similes, metaphors, analogies, and contrasts, which are a special kind of comparison. Great literature and great speeches abound with all four. The first two, similes and metaphors, are generally quite short—usually just "one-liners." They can enliven a speech.

Similes. Similes are short comparisons between unlike things using the words *like* or *as*. Often, they are only a sentence long—and sometimes only short phrases, such as *busy as a bee, hard as a rock, sharp as a tack, sweet as sugar*, or *straight as an arrow*. Similes appear often in literature, especially in poetry—for example, Robert Burns's "My love is like a red, red rose." Many proverbs and wise sayings are expressed as similes—for example, "Words spoken well and at the right time are like apples of gold in a setting of silver."

An expert on raising children who wants to make the point that shouting is not an effective means of discipline uses this simile: "Shouting to make your children obey is like using the horn to steer your car, and you get about the same results." A Wall Street stockbroker emphasizing just how rapidly things move on the floor of the stock exchange says, "Operating on the floor at Wall Street is like being in an avalanche where you have to run for your life." A psychologist speaking on dealing with trouble in one's life uses a simile and then expands upon it: "A small trouble is like a pebble. Hold it too close to your eye, and it fills the whole world and puts everything out of focus. Hold it at proper viewing distance, and it can be examined and properly classified. Throw it at your feet, and it can be seen in its true setting, just one more tiny bump on the pathway of life."

Metaphors. A metaphor is a short comparison between unlike things, based on resemblance or similarity, without using the words *like* or *as*. In other words, remove *like* or *as* from a simile and you have a metaphor. The similes used in the previous section can be expressed metaphorically: She's a busy bee. He's a straight arrow. It's just a pebble of trouble (on life's beach). Aristotle defined a metaphor as the act of giving a thing a name that belongs to something else. Sometimes the metaphor catches on. During the mid-1900s, Winston Churchill used the term *iron curtain* as a metaphor describing the line between Soviet and non-Soviet control. The term appears in dictionaries today with Churchill's meaning attached.

Why use metaphors? First, they enliven ordinary language and catch audience attention. Second, they encourage visualization and involvement by the audience. Third, they are efficient; they give much meaning with few words. A student says, "My dorm is a prison." The audience thinks: bad food, locked up, deprived of pleasures, cramped living, and other things.

One caution: avoid mixed metaphors—the awkward and often silly use of two metaphors together. Here are some examples:

- Burning the midnight oil at both ends.
- Grasping the straw that broke the camel's back.
- It's time to step up to the plate and cut the mustard.
- He swept the rug under the carpet.
- She grabbed the bull by the horns and ran with it.
- It's not rocket surgery.
- You'll get in hot water skating on thin ice.
- We'll tackle that bridge when we come to it.

Analogies. Analogies or longer comparisons relate several similarities between objects and situations. Just as with examples, analogies may be real (literal) or invented (figurative). A politician uses a real, or literal, analogy when he claims that if a lottery works in Georgia, then it would work in Alabama. He compares the two states—both southern, similar geography, same types of people, same educational background and needs, and many other things—to show similarity. Literal analogies compare like things: man to man, flower to flower, machine to machine, sports activity to sports activity, city to city, country to country. Sometimes they are just a few sentences long; sometimes they may be several hundred words or even longer.

Figurative, or invented, analogies compare objects and events that fall into unlike classes by stating a relationship between them. Since figurative analogies are invented or imagined, they don't provide hard evidence. But because they are creative, figurative analogies can interest the audience and grab their attention. A teacher plans to lecture to her class about the importance of controlling their anger and not saying things they would later regret. She considers using the following simile: "Saying things in anger you will later regret is like driving nails in a fence. You can pull the nails out, but the scar remains." Then she decides the comparison would grab students' attention and have more effect if she extended it into a longer analogy. So she tells the following story.

"There was once a little boy who would often explode in anger and say things he later regretted. His father gave him a bag of nails and told him that every time he said something in anger that he later regretted, he should hammer a nail in the fence. The first day, the boy drove 16 nails into the fence. A week later, he drove only 7 nails. A month later, he would go several days without having to pound a nail in the fence. He discovered it was easier to control his anger than to drive nails into the hardwood fence. He explained this to his father, who suggested that the boy pull out one nail each day he was able to control his anger. Months later, the nails were all gone. The father congratulated his son but pointed out the holes remaining in the fence. The father told the boy, 'When we get angry, we have a choice. We can hold our tongue or say things we later regret and leave scars just like those in the fence. It won't matter how many times we say I'm sorry; the wound is still there. A verbal wound is as bad as a physical one. When we get angry and say things we later regret, the damage has already been done.'"

Here's another example of how the vice president of sales of a large company—the Acme Company—used a figurative analogy to motivate his sales force during a very crucial time for the company.

"Back in the days when football coaches were able to instill true fear in their players, one of the toughest men to ever coach the game had his team ahead by six points with less than two minutes to play. The coach sent his quarterback in with instructions to play it safe and run out the clock. The quarterback came into the huddle and said, 'The coach says we should play it safe, but that's what the other team is expecting. Let's give them a surprise.' So he called a pass play. He dropped back and threw, and the defending cornerback, a national sprint champion, knifed in, intercepted, and headed for a touchdown. The quarterback knew he had a problem. He had to catch that cornerback or face his angry coach. The quarterback was no runner, but he took off after the fleet-footed cornerback, ran him down from behind on the five-yard line, and saved the game. After the game, the opposing coach came up to the coach noted for his toughness and said, 'What's this business about your quarterback not being a runner? He ran down my speedster from behind.' 'Yea,' said the tough coach, 'but your man was running for six points. My man was running for his life.'

"Now we are in the same situation here at Acme Company. It's not business as usual. We still have the lead in this year's sales, but our competitor has taken the ball, passed us in this month's sales, and is running hard. We are running for our life. But if each of you puts in the effort that you are capable of, we can catch them and hold on to our lead."

Contrasts. Contrasts differ from the three preceding forms of comparison in that they compare or appraise with respect to differences rather than similarities. Contrast involves two objects, conditions, or ideas that in some way or ways oppose each other. Similes, metaphors, and analogies support points by pointing out likenesses to another idea, object, or situation, whereas contrasts point out differences between two ideas, objects, or situations. Here is a contrast between winners and whiners.

- Whiners say, "I don't know, and neither does anybody else." Winners say, "Lets find out."
- Whiners make mistakes and say, "It's not my fault." Winners make mistakes and say, "I'm responsible, and I'm going to see what can be done to set things right."
- Whiners make promises and keep them if they feel like it. Winners make promises and keep them.
- Whiners say, "That's the ways it's always been. Why change?" Winners say, "There ought to be a better way to do it."
- Whiners say, "That's not my job." Winners feel responsible for doing more than the job requires.
- Whiners say, "I'm not as bad as a lot of other people." Winners say, "I'm going to try to improve." (*Source unknown*)

Exercise   Comparisons as Supporting Material

1. Look at a current newspaper, and select several articles. See how many comparisons you can find—similes, metaphors, analogies, and contrasts. Do the same thing with textbooks on literature, social science, and the physical sciences. What differences do you notice? What may account for these differences?

2. Listen carefully for comparisons people use in everyday conversation. Make note of them so you can share them with others in your class or training group. You will most likely find comparisons to be more common than you thought.

Guidelines for Using Comparisons

These guidelines can help you use comparisons effectively.

1. *Make them clear.* As with definitions, comparisons must be understandable to the audience. Make sure that the thing you are comparing something to is familiar with the audience. For example, comparing a windlass with a winch or a block and tackle with a pulley hoist will not be useful for most audiences.

2. *Avoid trite or shopworn comparisons.* Trite phrases are phrases that were once effective but now have become boring and at times even meaningless from overuse. Trite phrases are like pieces of merchandise everyone handles but no one buys. They are shopworn; they lack freshness and originality. "Blind as a bat" and "eat like a pig" are examples of trite expressions. Metaphors and images that at first appeal and evoke interest after much use may become dull and meaningless.

3. *Make sure comparisons are needed.* If they don't add support or clarify the point a speaker is trying to make, then they take time and do little else. In fact, they may do more harm than good. Brevity is a requirement for briefings and is a virtue in most speaking. In some situations, adding comparisons or any other unneeded supporting material increases length at a cost too great to pay.

4. *Make certain literal comparisons are between similar items.* For example, a speaker wishes to make the point that because a program worked in another city it should work in his city. However, one city has a high cost-of-living index, the other, low; one city has 1 million people, the other, 50,000; and one city is in the northeastern United States, the other, in the South. In this case, he is comparing two dissimilar cities and is not very likely to adequately support his point.

5. *Ensure that listeners easily understand the similarity between two objects.* This is especially important with figurative comparisons. You understand when a speaker says, "Buying too many groceries is like eating too much food—in one case, the refrigerator is too full; in the other case, you are." On the other hand, a speaker might say, "Buying too many groceries is like buying too much gasoline—in one case, the refrigerator is too full; in the other case, your car won't hold it." There may be some logic for the last comparison, but by the time you figure it out, it's too late; the speaker is talking about something else. If the speaker has to take the time to explain the comparison, time is wasted and the effect is lost.

Check Yourself: What Have You Learned?

- ☑ Supporting material holds listeners' attention and helps them understand, remember, and accept a speaker's points.

- ☑ Definitions, examples, and comparisons can be used as clarification support.

- ☑ Definitions establish a common ground for understanding key terms and phrases.

- ☑ Definitions are important because
  a. sometimes words sound like other words.
  b. sometimes words are new.
  c. words often have more than one meaning.
  d. different words can mean the same things.
  e. emotional meanings of some words overshadow the intended meaning.
  f. meanings of words change over time.

- ☑ Definitions may be short or extended, and they may explain the meaning of acronyms, define words according to classification, or define words operationally.

- ☑ Examples clarify and help listeners understand and group abstract or difficult ideas.

- ☑ Examples may be short (instances) or long (illustrations), real or invented.

- ☑ Examples should be representative, clear, relevant, appropriate, and interesting; they can be personalized, short, and clustered together.

- ☑ Comparisons include similes, metaphors, analogies, and contrasts (the opposite of comparisons).

- ☑ Comparisons should be clear, not trite, and needed. Literal ones must share similarities; for figurative ones, the comparison must be apparent.

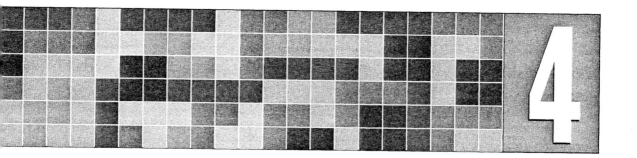

Using Proof Support

OBJECTIVE

- To comprehend how to use proof support in a presentation

TASKS

- Differentiate between expert and peer testimony and tell how to use each.
- Discuss the types of statistics, and give guidelines for using them.
- List the general tests for evaluating verbal material.
- Explain the place of emotional and logical appeals in speaking.

In addition to definitions, examples, and comparisons—types of clarification support discussed in Chapter 3—two other types of support—statistics and testimony—can also serve as clarification support. These two types also share another function. Statistics and testimony are generally the strongest proof support speakers can offer in support of claims or positions they advocate. Therefore, statistics and testimony are especially useful when speakers are seeking to advocate or persuade. This chapter discusses proof support and gives the six general tests for all verbal supporting material (clarification and proof). Finally, it treats the use of emotional appeals with verbal supporting materials.

TESTIMONY

Listeners are interested in two types of testimony—expert testimony and peer testimony. Words and thoughts of experts are particularly useful when you wish to add strong proof support for assertions or points that you make. No one is expected to be an expert on all subjects; speakers must often rely on what others have said. At times, testimony of others is used simply to clarify or explain an idea; often, it is intended to provide proof for a claim. Speakers may directly quote the words of the expert, or they may paraphrase or put what the speaker said in their own words, being careful not to distort the original meaning. Sometimes, speakers may choose to use peer testimony rather than expert testimony for support.

Expert Testimony

Expert testimony must satisfy more demanding criteria than peer testimony.

If you are presenting a talk on managerial effectiveness in an organization, one of your main points might be the importance of effective downward communication. In other words, you want to stress how important it is for supervisors to keep their subordinates informed. You might quote from a study conducted by an authority and reported in a leading trade journal that says: "Managers and supervisors have an increased responsibility to keep subordinates informed." You might also report published findings showing that "face-to-face communication, including group meetings and one-on-one dialogue," proved the most effective means of communicating with employees. Sometimes, you will want to use direct quotations or verbatim testimony as in the preceding examples. At other times, you will paraphrase or put in your own words what another has said.

A speaker talking about the importance of education in his state says, "Make no mistake about it—our elected officials believe education is important. Here's what the governor said last week: 'Education is my number one priority. It always has been and it always will be.' Just this morning the headline in the morning paper said 'Most state legislators place education first.'" It's clear the speaker quoted both the governor and the newspaper. The speaker might have instead paraphrased them: "Make no mistake about it—our elected officials believe education is important. The governor recently said that education is his number one priority, and most state legislators agree." Paraphrasing often allows us to simplify or make the information easier to digest without changing its meaning.

No matter whether a source is quoted or paraphrased, it must pass two tests to determine credibility: (1) Is the source truly expert? In other words, is the source of information competent on the given subject? For example, an NBA basketball player may be expert in basketball but probably not on what kind of automobile you should buy. (2) Is the source trustworthy? That is, can the source be trusted to be honest and unbiased? A source may be competent or expert but might not meet the criterion of trustworthiness. For example, suppose a government is interested in the amount and types of chemical weapons possessed by an enemy country. The leader of the enemy country is most likely an expert concerning his country's storehouse of chemical weapons, but would you trust him to tell you the correct information? Probably not. On the other hand, a source might be trustworthy but not expert. For example, your Uncle Carl might be a man of perfect integrity, trustworthy in all regards. But he most likely doesn't have a clue concerning the chemical weapons possessed by the enemy country in question. Neither the leader of the country nor your Uncle Carl would be good sources of information on the subject. One is not trustworthy; the other, not expert. A valid source must be both expert and trustworthy.

While it's important that *you as speaker* believe your expert testimony comes from credible sources, it is even more important that your audience considers the sources you use credible—that is, both expert and trustworthy. If the audience does not automatically accept the source as credible, consider not using the source. If you plan to use it anyway, be ready to tell the audience why the source deserves acceptance. Remember, also, that audiences vary. One audience might consider a certain source credible, whereas another would not. Know your audience.

INSIGHT

"I don't know who the source is, but I liked what he had to say."

—Reply from a student when asked to give background about a questionable source

---

Peer Testimony

Not only are listeners interested in the testimony of experts, but they also like to hear the opinions of persons like themselves. In a democracy especially, we value the opinion of the common person. This explains why so many news stories feature "man on the street" interviews with men and women just like us. *Although not strong proof support, the opinions of others influence us.* And although peer testimony doesn't need to meet the same rigid criteria for expertness that expert testimony must meet, trustworthiness is important. For peer testimony to be effective, the audience must consider the peers or common people quoted or paraphrased to be trustworthy.

Guidelines for Using Testimony

Ask yourself the following questions as you choose testimony to support a point:

- If using expert testimony, is the source credible—that is, truly expert and trustworthy?
- If using peer testimony, is the source trustworthy—that is, honest, believable, and respected?
- If using a direct quotation, is it accurately quoted?
- Is the quotation short and to the point?
- Have you made it clear to the audience whether you are paraphrasing or quoting directly?
- If paraphrasing, have you done so accurately without distorting the intent of the source?
- If quoting directly, have you accurately attributed the testimony prior to the quote?
- If quoting directly, have you clearly signaled where the quotation begins and ends?
- Is the testimony relevant? Clear? Interesting?
- Will the testimony help the listener understand?

Exercise   Credible Testimony

Compile a list of names that are currently in the news, such as the president of the United States, the Senate majority leader, the Senate minority leader, your congressional representative and senators, or your state governor and other elected state and local officials. Also include religious leaders and leaders of activist groups, such as those advocating gay rights or the ethical treatment of animals. Include movie and television stars, well-known professional athletes, CEOs of major corporations, and others in the news. Then think of several audiences that you might be called upon to speak to—college students, your colleagues at work, business leaders in your area, local Republican or Democratic organizations, and so forth. Decide which personalities would be most credible with each organization and explain why.

STATISTICS

Statistics are perhaps the most misused and misunderstood type of verbal support. When properly collected and wisely used, statistics can help speakers clarify their ideas. Statistics are also the most powerful proof support a speaker can use. However, *not all figures are statistics*; some are simply numbers. Statistics show relationships, largeness or smallness, or increases or decreases, or they summarize large collections of facts or data.

Statistics—a lot of numbers looking for an argument.

INSIGHT

—W. Kilbride

Types of Statistics

Statistics can be classed according to three major functions they perform as support material: magnitude, segments, and trends.

Magnitudes. Statistics describe the scope of a problem or situation in a compressed space. Statistical description of magnitude when complemented by an analogy helps an audience understand the significance of a problem or issue. For example, a teacher teaching on "Water Use in the United States" seizes on a statistic she read in the morning paper reporting that an estimated 1 million gallons of water was used to extinguish a fire in town. She says to the students, "Do you know how much water 1 million gallons is? If you use 50 gallons each time you take a bath, it's enough to take 20,000 baths—or one bath a day for nearly 60 years. It's enough to fill a swimming pool 267 feet long, 50 feet wide, and 10 feet deep. If you drink eight cups of water each day of your life, you'd have to live about 700 years to drink 1 million gallons of water."

Segments. Statistics can be a useful tool for isolating parts of a problem or issue to show what parts of the problem are caused by certain factors. Segmenting is especially useful with very complex subject matter, where breaking the problem down can help the audience understand each part and therefore the whole problem. But segmenting is also useful in making a simple point. A United Way campaign worker talking to a local Rotary Club wanted to dispel the notion that people with lower incomes give proportionately less to the United Way than people with higher incomes. He said, "We surveyed our contributors last year. For those earning $25,000 to $50,000, the average gift was 1 percent of their income. Those earning $50,000 to $75,000 gave slightly less. Those earning $75,000 to $100,000 gave slightly over 1 percent. In other words, there was little difference in percent given. In fact, the lowest-paid group gave slightly more than the next group." In other words, people from different incomes give the same proportion—an average gift of 1 percent of their income.

Trends. Statistics are especially useful for describing trends over time. A division chief briefs the vice president of his company concerning a need to increase his division's budget. "Twenty years ago our budget was $5 million. Today it is $10 million, but the price of doing business has tripled in that time. In other words, our budget has not kept up with inflation." A nutritionist talking on "Obesity in America" says, "Obesity—30 pounds overweight for a 5'4" person—is on the rise. Twenty years ago, only 3 states reported over 15 percent of its population as obese. Ten years ago, 20 states reported over 15 percent. Today, every state counts over 15 percent as obese. In 20 states, nearly one fourth of the citizens are obese. We have a serious nutrition problem in America."

Guidelines for Using Statistics

When you use statistics, ask yourself these questions. The answers will help you determine whether the statistics are good ones to use.

1. *Are the statistics recent?*   Figures concerning the cost of living in 1980 would have limited usefulness for today's family planning its budget. When selecting statistics to use, be on guard if no date is given or if the statistics are outdated. A student giving a speech on "Computers in America" reports that 53 percent of American homes have personal computers. While it is not always necessary for speakers to tell the origin of the statistic, especially if the speaker is an expert or the statistic is well known, in this case the speaker should have supplied the information. He could have said, "According to the *New York Times Almanac*, 53 percent of homes have personal computers." But in this case, still more information is needed, for this statistic came from the 2002 edition of the *Almanac*. Furthermore, the statistic is for the year 2000. What he could have said is, "According to the *New York Times Almanac*, in the year 2000, 53 percent of American homes had personal computers." But if his reason for the statistic was to show current computer ownership, he should have used the most recent edition of the *Almanac*. Or perhaps he could have gone on-line to find a more current statistic, but remember the cautions given near the end of Chapter 1 about using information from the Internet.

Of course, recency of the statistic may not be important in other cases. A study completed in 1946 on American casualties in World War II may be as accurate as one done today, perhaps more so. And a speech or report on "Life in the Twentieth Century" would benefit from giving statistical data compiled during the past century.

2. *Do the statistics indicate what they purport to?*   A single test score may not be a true measure of a student's ability. The number of planes may not indicate the strength of the Air Force. The membership of a church may not indicate the number of active congregants. Sometimes it is difficult, even impossible, to determine what a statistic really shows.

Some years ago, several studies reported the effects of antihistamines on colds. Each of the studies showed independently that a large percentage of colds cleared up after treatment. Advertising agencies grabbed the results and ran with them. Sales of antihistamines increased. Of course, what nobody mentioned was that a large percentage of the colds cleared up without treatment. As somebody pointed out years before, proper treatment cures a cold in seven days; left to itself, a cold will last a week.

3. *Do the statistics cover a long enough time or contain enough samples to be reliable?* The results of how one class responded to a new curriculum change would be less meaningful than how three or four classes responded to the change. A comparison of the general well-being of people in this decade with that of the last decade would be invalid because we have all of last decade to look at but this one isn't finished yet. Of course, if we are comparing well-being now to that 10 years ago, we would be able to arrive at statistics for a valid comparison.

Try flipping a coin 10 times. Chances are it will *not* come up heads five times and tails five times. But if you flip it 100 times, it will generally come out about 50-50. And if you flip it 1,000 times, you will have a nearly even split between heads and tails. When choosing statistics, take a hard look to make sure they cover a long enough time period.

4. *Is the sample representative? If the statistics are drawn from a sample, does the sample accurately represent the group to which you are generalizing?* A study reports that 20 years later, the average graduate of a certain MBA program is making a salary well into six figures. But wait. Were researchers really able to find all the graduates? Did they have addresses for all of them? And did all the graduates respond? The researchers almost certainly didn't find all of them. Furthermore, it's a fact that usually less than half of the people asked ever respond to a survey. Also, the more successful graduates most likely hold higher-profile positions and would therefore be easier to find and might be more likely to respond.

Earlier I mentioned "man on the street" interviews—information gained from men or women in the mall, at work, or in the marketplace. What these people say is interesting but not necessarily representative. Not everybody goes to the mall, or to work, or to the marketplace. Survey researchers still point to the great *Literary Digest* fiasco of 1936. Based on a representative survey of its 10 million subscribers, the *Digest* concluded that the Republican candidate for president, Landon, would receive more than twice as many electoral votes as the Democratic candidate, Roosevelt. Yet Roosevelt won by a landslide. How could this discrepancy happen with a random sample? Here's how—it was a telephone survey. In 1936 not everyone could afford a telephone or, for that matter, a subscription to *Literary Digest*. Economically, those surveyed were a special kind of people, a kind who tended to vote Republican. The sample elected Landon; the voters elected Roosevelt.

Researchers are now more sensitive to problems in obtaining a representative sample. They know we can only have statistical confidence in a purely random sample. Unfortunately, a random sample is generally too difficult and expensive to obtain; therefore, marketing research relies on stratified random sampling. The population is categorized—a representative number of Whites, Blacks, Hispanics, men, women, Protestants, Catholics, Jews, northeasterners, midwesterners, southerners, westerners, and so forth. All the while, the group must also be stratified according to education, age, and other relevant factors. Then, once researchers identify their sample, they randomly select people who fit the criteria. For example, they have a certain number of white, Catholic, midwestern women over age 40 who have completed a master's degree and live on a farm. They randomly select one who meets all the criteria. But what happens if the targeted person can't be located or doesn't respond? They select another, and another, until one responds. But what if the researchers do their calling at evening between the hours of 7 and 9 P.M.? They have systematically eliminated persons who work the evening shift, go to night classes, or just don't stay home in the evening—and they have introduced bias into the sample.

Researchers are sensitive to the need of a sample to represent the larger population to which they generalize. Speakers need to have the same sensitivity as they choose statistics as support material for points they wish to make.

5. *When statistics report differences, are the differences significant?* The previous point suggests why differences may not be real or significant. That's why researchers often say something like "The poll shows candidate Smith and candidate Jones in a virtual tie. Candidate Smith has 42 percent of the vote; candidate Jones has 39 percent; the rest is undecided. The survey has an error factor of plus or minus 5 points." Even with precautions and allowance for margins of error, we've all seen cases where surveys were wrong. Be certain that variations can't be attributed to chance. In other words, if the statistics were collected again, would the results differ? How many times would you have to collect them to feel confident in the findings? Think back to the coin-flipping experiment. Better yet, try it and you will have a better understanding of this point and the three previous points.

6. *When comparing things, are the units of measure compared the same?* Failure in one course might have a different meaning than failure in another. If more students fail one course than another, you cannot necessarily conclude that the content of one course is more difficult. Perhaps the grading scale rather than the content was more difficult.

Think back to what was said in Chapter 3 about using comparisons—similes, metaphors, analogies, and contrasts. Statistics also compare things; they show relationships. Remember we said, "Statistics show relationships, largeness or smallness, or increases or decreases, or they summarize large collections of facts or data." Since statistics compare things or show relationships, much of what we said about selecting comparisons as support material also applies to statistics.

7. *Do the statistics come from a reliable source—one that's expert and trustworthy?* And is the source clearly indicated? It's more effective to state the source of the information than to preface the statistic with "recent surveys show" or "I read in the paper." Look again at the checklist for using testimony on page 72. Apply the relevant points as you select which statistics to use.

8. *Are the statistics likely to aid listener understanding?* Could visual aids be used to present the statistics in graphic or tabular form for easier understanding? (We'll discuss visual aids in Chapter 6.) Have figures been rounded off where possible? Listeners are more likely to remember "nearly $45,000" than "$44,871.24." Is the number of statistics limited so they don't overwhelm listeners? Could the significance of statistics be made clearer with meaningful comparisons? To say that World War II cost the United States $200 billion would not be as clearly perceived as if the figures were converted to today's dollars or if they were compared to the cost of a war today using a standard measure. Statistics not only must support the point but also must illuminate or aid understanding.

He uses statistics as a drunk uses a street lamp, only for support and not for illumination.

—Andrew Lang

INSIGHT

---

9. *Have you interpreted the statistics for the audience?* Have you drawn from the statistics an inference to the point you are making? Often, speakers use statistics but don't explain what the statistics mean.

An agribusiness speaker tells a group of Iowa farmers, "This was a strong year for corn production. The United States produced 9.5 billion bushels of corn this year. Next year may be better." That's a nice figure to know, but the listeners may be wondering, "So what does that mean?" The speaker, knowing that interpretation may be in order, says, "This means that for corn production to be profitable, we must find more uses for corn." And the farmers are thinking, "That's right! And are we?" The speaker continues. He uses the 9.5 billion figure and the projection for even more production next year as a bridge to a discussion of innovations under way to find more uses for corn.

The speaker continues, "Work is under way in many areas. For example, we are extracting derivatives from corn, which will lead to expansion of the use of ethanol. And we are also developing such products as antifreeze and various food products, which could account for consumption of an additional 500 million corn bushels annually. Furthermore, work is progressing well to produce a corn-based chemical in the production of commercial plastics—a use that may require 200 million bushels of corn annually. And the list goes on."

Notice how the speaker interprets the statistic. He tells what it means. He draws an inference from the statistic to the point he makes that "we must find more uses for corn." Effective use of statistics almost always requires speakers to interpret them for the audience—to tell what they mean, to show how they support the point they are making. But interpretation is important with all means of support. Be careful when assuming listeners will know what the support means. Draw an inference from the support to the point it supports. Tell what the support means.

10. *Finally, do the statistics make sense?*   Consider these quotations:

- "It weighed less than average, but it must be remembered that the average was higher than usual."—a British radio program
- "We look forward to the day when everyone will receive more than the average wage."—Australian minister of labor
- "Most people have more than the average number of television sets in their homes."—a speech to a communications conference

GENERAL TESTS FOR VERBAL MATERIAL

How do you decide what kinds of verbal supporting material—definitions, comparisons, examples, statistics, testimony—to use in a presentation when there is so much to choose from? The subject, purpose, and objective of your talk and the composition of your audience—factors discussed in Chapter 1— will help you determine the amount and kinds of support to use. The type of talk—informative, persuasive, entertaining (also discussed in Chapter 1)— will also influence your selection of supporting material. You will also want to vary the kinds of material used; seldom will you use only one type. While we have considered guidelines or questions to ask as you use each kind of verbal supporting material—definitions, examples, comparisons, testimony, and statistics—six general tests can be applied to all verbal supporting material. Each can be expressed by a single word.

Relevance.   As discussed earlier, each piece of support should relate or pertain to the point it attempts to support. Often, speakers find interesting or humorous stories or other material they can't resist using. While the story may engage the audience, if it isn't relevant it detracts from the presentation. Recently, a local veterinarian was giving a presentation on "Taking Good Care of Your Pet." His rather dull talk was not helped by his attempts at humor, most of it irrelevant.

While discussing the importance of not overfeeding fish, he said, "That reminds me of a story of little Jimmy. Little Jimmy was filling a hole in his garden when his neighbor looked over the fence and asked Jimmy what he was doing. 'My goldfish died and I'm burying him,' replied Jimmy tearfully. The neighbor said, 'That's an awfully big hole for a goldfish, isn't it?' As Jimmy patted down the last heap of dirt, he replied, 'That's because he's inside your stupid cat.'"

The story brought more groans than laughs, and listeners were left wondering what the story had to do with the importance of not overfeeding fish. While they were trying to make sense of the story, the speaker went on to another subject, and both listening and comprehension by the audience suffered. Make sure your supporting material is relevant.

Variety. Presentations should not rely excessively on one or two types of support material. Instead, use several types of support—definitions, examples, comparisons, testimony, and statistics. Use different forms also—instances and illustrations, similes and analogies, expert testimony and peer testimony. Perhaps you will also choose to use humor and visual support (discussed in the next two chapters). Strive for variety in the support material you use in your presentations. It enlivens presentations and helps hold audience interest.

Amount. Include a sufficient amount of support material to make the ideas both clear and compelling to the audience. One of the most difficult things for beginning speakers is to find enough good support material. On the other hand, it's possible to use too much supporting material. Some speakers tell story after story, without making their point. This behavior may be justified if the sole purpose is to entertain, but if the audience expects information, then the speaker has failed.

Detail. Each piece of support needs to be developed to the extent that listeners can both understand the support and see how it backs up the point it supports. Look again at what was said earlier in this chapter about interpreting or drawing inferences from statistics to the points they support. The same is true for all supporting material. Interpret or explain your support so listeners clearly understand why you used it.

Appropriateness. Each piece of material must be appropriate for the audience, the speech, and the occasion. For example, a funeral oration is probably not the time to tell a joke, though a humorous illustration or anecdote from the person's life might be appropriate. In military briefings, humor is seldom appropriate. A factual report on company earnings for the past year would probably not contain peer testimony, though expert testimony would most likely be very appropriate. And if you feel a certain piece of supporting material might offend your audience, reconsider its use. A good rule to follow is this: *If you don't know if it is appropriate, don't use it.*

Logicality. Logical thinking should back verbal support. Some contend that emotional support appeals to listeners more strongly than does logical support. They point out that the most effective persuasive speeches rely heavily on emotional appeals. This is true. But this point is important: *The dichotomy between logical and emotional appeals is false.* Logic and emotion go hand in hand. An emotional appeal may be backed by strong logic. I may become emotional about things I have logically thought through, such as love of my country or devotion to my family. Do not confuse illogicality or irrationality with emotionality. Emotional appeals often complement and strengthen both clarification and proof support.

EMOTIONAL APPEALS

There are times when listeners are not guided by reason. They may not be moved by an example or persuaded by a comparison. Even a statistic or testimony from a credible source may fail to convince them. When the time is appropriate, there is nothing immoral or wrong with appealing to emotion. Although there are many types of emotions, here are 10 common ones. Discover which emotions move your listeners, and you will hold their attention and gain their acceptance.

Love. Love may be directed toward a spouse, parents, children, friends, and others. Here is an example of an appeal to love: "Certainly you love your family and want to be sure they are cared for if you die. Term insurance is the answer. Term insurance provides the most coverage for the least money. And our company has the lowest rates anywhere. Let me tell you how you can provide for your loved ones for just pennies a day." Love also extends to those we don't know. It's the motive for sending food to other countries, working in a shelter for the homeless, or feeling compassion for those less fortunate than us.

Hatred. You may hate personal enemies who have hurt you or enemies of your country. Or, a national leader may use insult, contempt, or ridicule to arouse passions against an enemy: "This attack upon our people shall not go unpunished. The thugs of this world cannot, will not, be allowed to run roughshod over the freedoms of peace-loving people. We shall pursue the perpetrators of this infamous crime to the ends of the earth. We will bring them to justice." This kind of statement effectively stirs the emotions. The more effectively you activate the emotions of your audience, the stronger your power to persuade them becomes.

Mirth.   Of all the emotions, mirth most likely brings an audible response—laughter. Many people who are too ashamed to cry in public will laugh with the slightest provocation. Humorous definitions and quotations and longer illustrations occur frequently in entertaining speeches. But sometimes a one-liner also causes a chuckle: "If everything is coming your way, you may be in the wrong lane." Most audiences enjoy appropriate humor. (Chapter 5 tells how to use humor effectively.)

Grief.   Abraham Lincoln appealed to grief in his Gettysburg Address when he said, ". . . in a larger sense, we cannot dedicate—we cannot consecrate—we cannot hallow this ground. The brave men, living and dead, who struggled here, have consecrated it far above our poor power to add or detract. . . . It is for us, the living, rather to be dedicated here to the unfinished work which they who fought here have thus so nobly advanced." Lincoln aroused audience emotion and went on to urge the audience to support his war plans. By sharing the emotion of grief with his audience, Lincoln took advantage of it to call for their support of his action.

Pride.   Leaders appeal to subordinates' pride in the company. The implied message is, "You share my pride in the company so you will work hard to make it profitable." Parents appeal to children to have pride in their room or in their abilities. The message is, "You have enough pride to keep your room clean and study hard to achieve success." Pride keeps people from quitting when discouraged. Appealing to the emotion of pride helps encourage work and productivity.

Shame.   Shame leaves a feeling that we have been disgraced or that others think poorly of us. The regret that may follow can lead to repentance and resolution to do better. For example, the mayor of a city speaks to his constituents: "The incident last week in our mall where four youths attacked an old man while scores of people stood and watched unwilling to assist—unwilling even to use a cell phone and call for help—should cause us all shame, whether we were there personally or not. The police cannot be everyplace. They need your help. To borrow the famous words of Todd Beamer, who did not stand by helplessly, 'Let's roll!'" Shame can be a powerful motivator in the right situation.

Hope.   Someone once said, "Without hope, you might as well give up." Hope is the expectation that things will get better. Hope motivates people to work so things do get better—hope of gain, development, improvement, and better economic times. A political leader tells campaign workers, "A month ago, they didn't give our candidate a chance. But yesterday's poll shows she gained 20 points in the last month. She is now within 8 points of the incumbent. If you will work as hard in the next two weeks as you have the last month, we'll have a new congressperson from this district." Hope causes us to lean forward and work toward a goal. Hope keeps people going.

Fear. People fear many things—pain, disease, death, poverty, even speaking in public. At the beginning of Chapter 1, I said, "Do you get nervous and fearful even *thinking* about the prospect of giving a speech or presentation? If so, you're not alone." Then I went on to say, "You may be unsure of your own speaking ability. But there is good news. You can be an effective speaker, the kind others admire—the kind who gets the job done in every speaking situation. This book will enable you to meet this objective." I appealed to fear, but I offered hope. Fear appeals are effective if they show a solution, if they offer hope.

Desire. We desire many things: wealth, possessions, achievement. Coaches of athletic teams appeal to the emotion of desire: "OK, men. How much do you want this win? We've played them twice this year. The first time we lost by one point. Just three weeks ago, we lost in overtime. Now here we are in the final game of the conference tournament. The winner advances; the loser stays home. How bad do you want to win? The team that wants this win the most will be the team that wins. I think you want it. And I think you'll get it."

Contentment. An appeal to contentment is nearly opposite to an appeal to desire. Appeal to contentment is appropriate if you want to avoid change. For example, a political campaigner says: "My fellow constituents. We've had four great years under Representative Andrews. You have more food on your tables, more money in your pockets, more jobs in the area, and a general feeling of prosperity. Let's send him back to Washington with an overwhelming mandate from his district." The speaker continues: "You share my feelings and emotions of contentment concerning Representative Andrews, so I know you will vote him back in office."

Exercise   Learning from Reading Speeches

Recognizing how others use supporting material will help you as you choose supporting material for your speeches. Since 1934, *Vital Speeches of the Day* has published important addresses that present varying viewpoints on a wide range of topics. Either examine a collection at a library or go to the website at www.votd.com and read several speeches. A word of caution: some use great supporting material; some do not. You decide how the ones you read did.

From time to time, newspapers print the text of important speeches, such as the president's State of the Union Address. Of course, you can search out speeches of most leading political leaders on-line. Select one or two to analyze. Notice how the speaker adapted supporting material to the audience.

A CONCLUDING OBSERVATION

Most principles and concepts discussed in Chapters 3 and 4 also apply to using humor as supporting material. Humorous support can take any one of the five forms discussed—definitions, examples, comparisons, testimony, and statistics. Many things discussed here also apply to the use of visual supporting material. Chapter 5 will treat humorous support, and Chapter 6 will consider visual support. But first, review what you have learned in this chapter.

Check Yourself: What Have You Learned?

- ☐ Testimony may come from experts or from peers.
- ☐ Expert testimony must be from competent and trustworthy sources.
- ☐ Peers must be considered trustworthy.
- ☐ Statistics show relationships—magnitudes, segments, and trends.
- ☐ These questions should be asked about statistics: Are they recent? Do they cover what they purport to? Do they cover a long enough time? Are they representative? Are they significant? Are similar things compared? Are they from a good source? Are they presented clearly? Are they interpreted for the audience? Do they make sense?
- ☐ General tests for supporting material are relevance, variety, amount, detail, appropriateness, and logicality.
- ☐ Emotional appeals should still be logical.

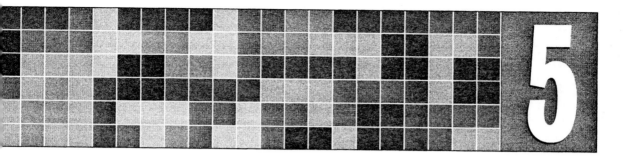

Using Humorous Support

OBJECTIVE

- To comprehend how to use humorous support in a presentation

TASKS

- Tell why humor can be effective support.
- Discuss the kinds of humorous support.
- Demonstrate how to use humor effectively.

Listeners admire speakers who use humor effectively, but many speakers are afraid to use humor except perhaps to gain audience attention at the beginning of a presentation. And most speakers who do attempt to use it in the body of a talk as supporting material do it poorly. Yet humor can be one of the most effective ways for speakers to illustrate and clarify their points.

WHY HUMOR IS EFFECTIVE

Although humor is usually not effective or appropriate in military or business briefings, research shows what experienced speakers know: in most speeches and classroom lectures, humorous supporting material regains attention, builds rapport, enhances speaker credibility, aids retention, and improves listening.

Humor Regains Attention

Humor can capture audience attention at the beginning of a presentation, which explains why so many speakers attempt to use humor to start their talks. Chapter 7 discusses the use of humor to gain initial audience attention. But humor is also very effective during the talk when audience attention wanes. The attention span of most people is at best a few minutes, so unless the material is very engaging, an audience's attention will wander. Humor regains their attention.

A speaker is using statistics to support his point that concern for the high salaries of major league baseball players is not new. He senses that audience attention is drifting, so he inserts a short example—a humorous instance—to support his point and also regain attention. He says, "Even back in 1930, players' salaries were often questioned. That year, Babe Ruth earned $80,000. When asked if he thought it was fair that he received more than President Hoover, he said, 'Well, I had a better year.' And he probably did. The point is this: the concern for salaries of ballplayers has been with us for a while." The speaker uses a witty instance to support his point and regain audience attention.

Humor Builds Rapport

Humor builds affinity and creates harmony with the audience. We like to laugh, and we like people who make us laugh. Humor is not laughter, but humor produces the physiological response of laughter. Just how much do we like humor? A lot, according to people with websites. The first search engine I tried yielded 10 million sites keyed to the word *humor*. Website owners key on humor because they know people like it. Stop and think about speakers you've heard recently. If they used humor well and appropriately (that is, you liked their humor) and if they made you laugh and feel good about being in their audience, you probably came away liking the speakers and what they said.

Audiences especially like speakers who can laugh at themselves when they flub up, mispronounce a word, or become tongue-tied. It happens to all speakers. I wish it didn't happen to me but it does, so I have lots of little lines I use, such as, "I just washed my mouth and can't do a thing with it" or "Did that sound as bad to you as it did to me?" or simply "That's not what I meant to say; let me try again." Of course, if it is a simple mispronunciation, just correct it, or if it is inconsequential, go on. You'll only show you're human.

Blessed are they who can laugh at themselves for they shall never cease to be amused.   **INSIGHT**

Humor Enhances Speaker Credibility

Studies show what experienced speakers know: speakers are rated as both more expert and more trustworthy (the two major aspects of credibility discussed in Chapter 4) when they use humor effectively. First, we believe that people who use humor are more relaxed and confident about the subject, so we judge them to be more competent or expert. Second—because we trust people we like, and because we like people who use humor—if all else is equal, we rate people who use humor as more trustworthy than those who don't. Of course, speakers must fit their humor to the audience. We tend to think people who use our kind of humor are more like us, and we put more trust in people who are similar to us.

Humor Aids Retention

People may come away from a speech unable to remember the main points, but they may remember the speaker used a "cute line about Babe Ruth and President Hoover." Many experienced speakers have certain humorous stories they use often because they know these particular stories are effective in helping audiences remember a point. The supporting material doesn't have to evoke strong laughter. It doesn't always need a punch line. When an illustration portrays a husband and wife miscommunicating because circle drive meant one thing to one and something else to the other, audiences remember it. Why? Because they see the humor of a man and woman going back and forth from circle drive to circle drive in their attempts to meet each other.

Humor Improves Listening

Watch an audience. Attention picks up and listening improves when speakers use humor. Speakers know listening improves when they give a funny definition, use a humorous illustration, or draw a witty comparison. They can see it on their listeners' faces. An expert fisherman reels them in with a quick definition of habitat as "a place where a particular species of fish was last week." An expert on physical fitness who is making the point that people want to be fit, but not bad enough to watch what they eat, tells this story: "A generously overweight man who had just finished working out got on the scales and exclaimed to his friend, 'I don't believe it. I started my diet yesterday, worked out today, and I'm heavier than I was before I started. Here, Fred, hold my jacket. Wow! I'm still heavier. Here, Fred, you'd better hold my Coke and my Twinkies, too.'" A political candidate who accuses his opponent of "all talk and no action" draws this comparison: "I feel like the old man who went to a hearing specialist who recommended a hearing aid. The man said, 'No way, I'm 97 years old, and I have already heard enough.'"

KINDS OF HUMOROUS SUPPORT

We can place humorous support into the same classes as general verbal support—definitions, examples, comparisons, testimony, and statistics. Furthermore, the types, suggestions, guidelines, checklists, and explanations given in the previous chapter also apply to humorous support.

INSIGHT	*"Laugh and the world laughs with you."*
	—Ella Wheeler Wilcox

Definitions

Definitions may be short or long. Many humorous definitions are one-liners designed not so much to define a term as to make us think about some aspect of the subject or point a speaker wishes to make: "Laughter is a frown turned upside down." "Love may be blind, but marriage is an eye-opener." "Egotism can be defined as obesity of the head." "An economist is a man who figures out tomorrow why the things he predicted yesterday didn't happen today." "Hypocrites are people who never intend to be what they pretend to be." "A lady is a woman who makes a man behave like a gentleman."

The preceding definitions most likely will not evoke laughter, but each is witty and can make a listener smile. A humorous definition can be useful if it helps clarify meaning while bringing a smile. But use caution. Humor should seldom take precedence over clarity. It should not detract from the definition.

Yet a humorous definition for humor's sake is at times acceptable, especially in speeches whose primary purpose is to entertain. A humorous definition may be acceptable even if its major purpose is to regain audience attention or build rapport or goodwill. For example, an instructor conducting a beginning training course on computers sees tension from the learners as they struggle with the new terminology. So the instructor says, "Don't let the terminology get you down. You'll learn it; until then, here are a few 'definitions' to consider:

- *BIT*:   a word used to describe computers, as in 'My computer cost quite a bit.'
- *BUG*:   what your eyes do after you've been staring at the computer screen for more than five hours.
- *CHIPS*:   the fattening food computer users eat to avoid leaving their keyboards even for meals.
- *DISK*:   what goes out in your back after bending over a computer keyboard for five hours at a stretch.
- *ERROR*:   what you made the first time you walked into a computer showroom to 'just look.'
- *CURSOR*:   what you want to do when your computer freezes up.
- *RAM*:   what you instinctively do to the side of your computer when it's not doing what it should.
- *WINDOW*:   what you want to heave your computer out of."

Some would argue that such a list is a waste of time, but it's probably not. It builds rapport with the students and supports the point that computer technology has a language of its own. Furthermore, the instructor has demonstrated that she understands the difficulty students may be having in learning new meanings of words.

Examples

Listeners often remember humorous examples better than nonhumorous ones. The Babe Ruth example, the example of the generously overweight man, and the example in Chapter 3 about Freddy and the yucky pancakes were humorous. The Babe Ruth one was real; the other two were invented. Two were short examples or instances; the other was an extended example. Humorous examples are often invented, although at times they are real and may arise from the speaker's experience, like the circle drive story from Chapter 4 or like the Methodist pastor in Pennsylvania who used a true story to point out the importance of being very careful when reading something to an audience. He told of the time he was using John Wesley's Covenant Renewal Service on New Year's Eve, one line of which goes: "Let us bind ourselves with willing bonds to our covenant God." The way it came out was, "Let us bind ourselves with willing blondes."

INSIGHT	*The best sense of humor belongs to the person who can laugh at himself.*

The key to using humorous examples is to tell them so they support the point rather than detract from it. Therefore, the lead-in line and the words after the example that draw the inference or show its relevance are both important. Notice how the following speaker uses an illustration about a duck to motivate a sales force.

> Perseverance is important. Just because people tell you they're not interested doesn't mean they really aren't. Just because a clerk tells you it's not in stock doesn't necessarily mean they don't have it. Sometimes a clerk will tell you that rather than take the time or effort to get it. Learn a lesson from a duck. A duck walked into a restaurant and said to the waiter, "Give me a Pepsi!" The waiter gave the duck a Pepsi, which he promptly drank in one gulp. The duck then turned to the waiter and asked, "Got any popcorn?" The waiter answered, "Nope. Don't sell popcorn. Just Pepsi." The duck left the restaurant but returned the next day. "Give me a Pepsi," the duck said and promptly finished it in one gulp. Turning to the waiter, the duck asked, "Got any popcorn?" Annoyed, the waiter answered "Look, duck. I told you yesterday, we don't serve popcorn, just Pepsi. If you ask me again, I'm going to nail your beak to the bar." Once again, the duck left the restaurant but returned the next day. Upon reaching the counter, he shouted to the waiter, "Give me a Pepsi!" The waiter handed the duck a Pepsi and watched as the duck finished the entire drink in one gulp. Then the duck turned to him and asked, "Got any nails?" "No," the bewildered waiter answered. "We don't have any nails." To which the duck responded, "Got any popcorn?" The duck didn't give up. Neither should you. Perseverance pays off.

Comparisons

Even when using examples, speakers imply or invite comparison—comparison of audience members' situations with the ones in the examples. The motivational speaker invited the sales force to compare their perseverance with that of the duck. See how in the next situation, the speaker uses good lead-in lines as he clearly draws a comparison between the treatment an organization has received from the Bigbee Company and the way a barber was treated by a customer.

> I'm not saying Bigbee Company gave misinformation. What I am saying is Bigbee didn't give all the information. To make informed decisions, your organization needs all the relevant information. You probably feel much like a barber in my hometown. A man with a little boy came into the barbershop. After the man received the full treatment—shave, shampoo, manicure, haircut, and so forth—he placed the boy in the chair and said, "I'm going to buy a new pair of shoes while you get your haircut. I won't be gone long." When the boy's haircut was completed and the man hadn't returned, the barber said, "Looks like your daddy's forgotten all about you." "That wasn't my daddy," said the boy. "He just walked up, took me by the hand, and said, 'Come on, son, we're gonna get a free haircut!'" Bigbee has treated your organization in much the same way the man treated the barber. He didn't really give you any misinformation; he just didn't give you all the information. If you do business with our company, we'll see that you get all the information.

The use of the barbershop comparison to motivate a sales force reminds us of the humorous comparison about the quarterback and the intercepted pass used in Chapter 3. In both cases, the speakers used appropriate lead-in lines and also words after the story to draw a comparison between the story and an existing situation. In both cases, the humorous comparisons kept attention, built rapport, and aided retention.

Humor is the lubricating oil of a speech. It prevents friction and wins goodwill.   **INSIGHT**

Of course, humorous comparisons can be short. A husband and wife who frequently conduct marriage seminars cluster several humorous comparisons to point out differences between men and women: "A woman marries a man expecting he will change, but he doesn't. A man marries a woman expecting she won't change, and she does." "A man will spend $2 for a $1 item he wants; a woman will spend $1 for a $2 item she doesn't want, if it's on sale." "A woman knows all about her children—their dentist appointments, romances, best friends, favorite foods, secret fears, hopes and dreams. A man is vaguely aware of some short people living in the house."

This same couple also uses humorous comparisons when describing children: "You throw a little girl a ball, and it will hit her in the nose.

You throw a little boy a ball, and he will try to catch it—and it will hit him in the nose." "Boys' rooms are usually messy. Girls' rooms are usually messy, except it's a better-smelling mess." "Baby girls find Mommy's makeup and almost instinctively start painting their face. Baby boys find Mommy's makeup and almost instinctively start painting the walls." "Girls are attracted to boys, even at an early age. At an early age, boys are attracted to dirt." "Girls turn into women. Boys turn into bigger boys." They use these to make the point that even though we treat them equally, there are basic differences between boys and girls and between men and women.

Testimony

Sometimes a humorous quotation will help a speaker make a point. Often, knowing that a well-known person said something makes it funnier. Funny people often say funny things. In the following examples, attaching the name to the quote makes it funnier, especially if the audience is familiar with the person who said it.

- "I don't date women my age; there aren't any."—Milton Berle
- "I set out to play golf and shoot my age; I shot my weight instead."— Bob Hope
- I'd much rather be a woman than a man. Women can cry, they can wear cute clothes, and they are the first to be rescued off of sinking ships."—Gilda Radner
- "Last night I played a blank tape at full blast. The mime next door went nuts."—Stephen Wright
- "Pro and con are opposites, that fact is clearly seen. If *progress* means to move forward, then what does *congress* mean?"—Nipsey Russel
- "Graduation speeches were invented largely in the belief that college students should never be released into the world until they have been properly sedated."—Gary Trudeau
- "If the fans don't come out to the ballpark, you can't stop them."— Yogi Berra

Experienced speakers listen to other speakers, especially well-known ones, with an ear toward quoting them in their own speeches. A speaker used the following story to emphasize the importance of having vision and a sense of where an organization should be headed: "The Reverend Billy Graham tells of a time early in his ministry when he arrived in a small town to preach a sermon. Wanting to mail a letter, he asked a young boy where the post office was. When the boy had told him, Dr. Graham thanked him and said, 'If you'll come to the church this evening, you can hear me telling everyone how to get to heaven.' 'I don't think I'll be there,' the boy said. 'You don't even know your way to the post office.'" Since Reverend Graham has told this story on himself many times, it's both appropriate and meaningful when the speaker attributes the story to him.

When using testimony as humorous support, the reason for giving the source is usually because it adds to the humor in some way, either as with the short quotations or as with the longer story from Billy Graham. Of course, at times people say things that come out wrong, and the fact that a well-known person made the statement contributes to both its humor and its value as supporting material.

- "Hazards are one of the main causes of accidents."—U.S. Occupational Safety and Health Administration
- "Make sure everybody who has a job wants a job."—George H. W. Bush, during his first campaign for the U.S. presidency in 1988
- "Things are more like they are now than they have ever been."—President Gerald Ford
- "Bruce Stutter has been around for a while, and he's pretty old. He's 35 years old. That will give you some idea of how old he is."—Ron Fairly, San Francisco Giants broadcaster
- "China is a big country, inhabited by many Chinese."—French president Charles de Gaulle

It's not just what was said but who said it that makes it funny.	**INSIGHT**

Statistics

Let's face it—most statistics are dry, although some are entertaining but perhaps useless. For example: a regulation golf ball has 336 dimples, the world record for rocking nonstop in a rocking chair is 440 hours, Americans on the average eat 18 acres of pizza every day, and the earth weighs around 6,588,000,000,000,000,000,000,000,000 tons.

So how do you use humorous statistics to spice up a talk without giving useless ones that detract from the content? Here is an example. A physiologist speaking on "The Amazing Brain" said:

Of course, as magnificent as our brains are, we may wonder why people don't use theirs more. Sometimes people make decisions, and we wonder where their brain was. We may accuse people of making decisions using another part of their anatomy. We must remember the average human body contains 66 pounds of muscle, 42 pounds of bone, and only 3.5 pounds of brain. This may explain some muscle-bound, bonehead decisions people make. But seriously, isn't it amazing what the human brain can do?

Notice how the physiologist took common statistics and used them in a humorous way.

Sometimes speakers make humorous statistical comparisons. A football coach from a major university was talking to the Quarterback Club—a group of football enthusiasts—in a large city. The much-admired and good-humored president of the club, Tom, was a friend of the coach and the father of 11 children. In the talk, the coach said, "We hope to win all our regular games, win the playoffs, play in the bowl, and win it for the national title. That would be 13 wins. That's more wins than there are months in a year. That's even more wins than Tom has kids." This may not sound funny when you read it, but it's the kind of thing the folks at the Quarterback Club, a bunch of sports fans, will laugh at. The coach knew his friend would take the gibe good-naturedly, and he knew the audience would too.

A person about to give some startling statistics might prepare his audience like this:

Statistics can be made to say anything you want. For instance, research demonstrates that pickles cause cancer, airline tragedies and auto accidents, even death. About 99.9 percent of cancer victims have eaten pickles at some time in their lives. Nearly 100 percent of people driving cars and flying in airplanes have eaten them. And pickle eaters born in the eighteenth century have all died. So statistics can be deceptive. But I want you to know that the statistic I am about to give you involves no trickery. It is startling, and it is true.

Why would a speaker say this in introducing a statistic? First, the humor gets attention; the audience is primed to listen. Second, the speaker is telling the audience not to dismiss the statistic they are about to hear.

The effective use of statistics, especially humorous ones, depends on knowing the audience. And some of the most effective humor does not come with stories and incidents that come from elsewhere; it comes from situations. A speaker takes a drink of water, spills it on his tie, and then pokes fun at himself. An assistant accidentally knocks over a prop, sending it crashing to the floor, and the speaker explains, "Actually I have him do that so I can get your attention." And when I retired several years ago, a man who had been a close colleague before he left to take another position, returned to be my boss. His name was Lance Lord. The master of ceremonies at my retirement dinner said, "People always said John wouldn't retire until the Lord came again. I guess that's happened."

People make others laugh by calling attention to funny stuff around them.

HOW TO USE HUMOR

Many examples used in this book are humorous. But reading humorous examples to support a point is not the same as hearing them. Reading and hearing are not the same. The *lead-in* material when using humor in speaking is different from the lead-in material when using humor in writing. And words that follow humorous support or words used to draw an inference differ between written and spoken messages. So how do speakers use humor effectively in speeches? Here are 10 guidelines to consider when using humor as supporting material.

Set It Up

Audiences are ready to smile, chuckle, or laugh out loud when they know something funny is on the way. Speakers set the tone early in a speech. For example, at times I mention early in a speech that I grew up in Iowa. When talking to audiences outside the Midwest, I often say, "We talked funny back in Iowa. We drank pop (not sodas), warshed (not washed) our clothes, and fished in a crick (not a creek)." Then, later, when I tell a funny story about a lady who warshed her clothes in a crick, the audience is loosened up and ready to laugh even before I get to the punch line. At other times, just saying something humorous early in the speech builds audience expectation and the understanding that laughter is acceptable.

Time It

Timing here does not refer to the time in the speech to use humor (Chapter 7 tells how to use humor at the beginning of the talk and we've already seen how humor can support points throughout the speech). Here, timing means cadence, rhythm, or way the illustration, comparison, or statistic is communicated. Learn good timing by listening to experienced speakers. Timing is important with all support material and especially with humorous support. Many speakers don't time material well, leading to the comment: "Some people just can't tell stories." Timing is important with humor.

> A man who traveled around the country giving speeches went into a café in a town he was visiting and noticed a group of men seated around the table laughing. He decided to listen, hoping to pick up a few new stories to use in his speeches. He observed the men for

some time. The first man hollered "43," and the rest of them laughed. After the laughter subsided, the second yelled "197," whereupon the others nearly fell on the floor laughing. Then a third said "66." Again, the others laughed heartily. This continued until it was the last man's turn. He said "29," and nobody laughed. The sequence happened several times, with speakers calling out different numbers—110, 214, 9, 72, and so forth. Finally, the stranger asked his waiter, "I've been observing those men over at the corner table; I notice that one after another they yell out numbers and the rest of them laugh. Why is that?" "Well," said the waiter, "those men come in every morning to drink coffee and tell jokes. In fact, they've done it so long and know the jokes so well that they have numbered all the jokes. Then, rather than telling the joke, the one whose turn it is just hollers out the number, and the rest of them laugh." "That partly explains what is going on," said the out-of-towner, "but why don't they laugh when the last fellow yells out a number?" "Oh," said the waiter, "You know how it is. Some people just can't tell a joke."

Vitalize It

In Chapter 3, we discussed personalizing examples, both real and invented ones. Real examples and comparisons often possess vitality missing in invented ones. Constructed examples or hypothetical comparisons will have more vitality if they sound real—that is, as if they actually happened. Instead of saying, "I heard a story about a truck driver . . ." or "They tell about a meter man who . . ." consider putting the story into a real setting to add vitality. For example:

> A man from another city addresses a Lions Club. He tells them how much he admires their programs to help others, especially their program for saving sight. Then he continues, "I admire your team spirit and I'm pulling for your club in its future endeavors. In fact, I feel like a meter man in our town.
>
> "My wife and I live next door to an attractive couple with two small children. They are very health conscious and swim laps in their pool every morning. Normally after the swim, the lady just pulls a long housecoat over her swimming suit and busies herself with housework after her husband and children leave. This particular day, she had gone to the laundry room with a load of clothes to wash when she decided to knock down a spider web just outside the laundry room door. She couldn't quite reach it, so she grabbed her son's baseball bat. Fearing that the web might get in her hair, she also put on his football helmet, which was lying on the laundry room floor, and then took several mighty swipes with

the bat and brought it down—spider, web, and all. Without thinking, she whisked off her housecoat, picked the mess up, and was ready to walk back into the laundry room dressed only in her bikini and put the whole thing into the washing machine when she looked up and saw a very surprised man standing there reading the meter. He stammered, "Lady, I don't know what sport you are practicing for, but whatever it is, I'm pulling for your team." [Pause for laughter.] Lions, today I am pulling for your team."

Know the Item Thoroughly

We've all heard speakers stumble through a potentially humorous item or make it through the item in fine shape only to forget the punch line. But if speakers know the story and have told it before, they will be able to tell it again and know the kind of response to expect. It's generally a good rule not to use a story or humorous item of any kind in a speech unless you have told it several times in informal situations so you can both practice and gauge the reactions of others.

> A preacher was on vacation. He and his wife decided to visit a church near the resort where they were staying because they had heard the minister there was an outstanding speaker and a man of unquestioned moral integrity. So both the preacher and his wife were jolted when the minister began his sermon that day by saying, "I spent some of the best years of my life in the arms of another man's wife." In fact, the entire congregation was in shock. The minister had their undivided attention as he continued, "It was my father's wife, my mother."
>
> The visiting preacher thought that would be a good technique to gain his congregation's attention the next week, so he decided to use the item. Unfortunately, he hadn't practiced the item. The next week, the preacher began his sermon, "I spent some of the best years of my life in the arms of another man's wife." And he couldn't remember what came next, so he thought if he said the line again, perhaps he could remember. So he started over, "I spent some of the best years of my life in the arms of another man's wife." Again, he couldn't remember. Once more he started, "I spent some of the best years of my life in the arms of another man's wife." Finally, in frustration, he blurted out, "And I can't remember who she was."

It pays to know the item thoroughly, not only so you can remember the punch line, but also so you can tell it with ease and confidence. If you've practiced it, you will be able to anticipate audience response. You'll have the timing down. You'll know when to pause and which words to emphasize. For example, if you were using the previous item, you would probably want to deliver the punch line this way: [pause] "It was my father's [emphasize the word *father's*] wife [pause again], my mother [pause]." Knowing the item allows you to deliver it so you get the desired response.

Don't Laugh Before the Audience Does

First, when you laugh at something you said and the audience doesn't laugh, you look silly. Second, you seem focused on yourself rather than the audience. Third, the benefit gained from humor is from your words, not your reaction. This doesn't mean you need to keep a straight face or "deadpan." Stephen Wright is a comedian who uses deadpan to good advantage. An old-time comedian, Red Skelton, did just the opposite. He often laughed at his own jokes. Both comedians have been effective, but comedians use humor for its own sake. Speakers use humor to make a point.

Play on the Unexpected

We often laugh at things we don't expect. Years ago, streaking—a fad where individuals run naked in public places—hit college campuses. The reaction of most people was to laugh. As the behavior became more common, people either looked out of interest or were bored by the practice and it soon died out. Humor is much like streaking. When something unexpected is said, people laugh. When it becomes commonplace or unexpected, people are at best interested, perhaps bored. Here are several ways to play on the unexpected.

Exaggeration or overstatement.   A huge man on a large horse isn't funny, but place him on a small, balky donkey and the exaggeration will cause even the most matter-of-fact individual to smile. Grant Wood's *American Gothic* painting of a stern-looking farmer with a pitchfork and a wife who looks like her face will break if she smiles is humorous because the painter exaggerated certain features. In another example, a woman tells the story of a married couple having an argument. She makes the story more humorous with exaggeration: "I couldn't see who the woman was talking to at first. She completely blocked my view of her husband, sort of like a huge dump truck parked in front of a Volkswagen." She goes on to say, "The little man stood five foot four and weighed 110 pounds soaking wet; his wife looked like she threw the discus about 30 years and 100 pounds ago." The speaker's exaggeration makes us smile.

Puns or plays on words.   Puns are considered by many to be low humor, but they can be effective in gaining attention and making a point. Here are two short puns: (1) Show me a squirrel's home, and I'll show you a nutcracker suite. (2) Perhaps you've heard the story of the human cannonball in the circus. He told the boss he wanted to quit, and the boss said, "Please don't quit. I don't know where I could find another man of your caliber." Puns like these two short ones often bring groans, but when used effectively they can support a point. Here is a longer pun.

A speaker urges his company to reject a proposal. He tells this story: "Three animals were having a huge argument over who was the best. The first, a hawk, claimed that because of his ability to fly, he could attack anything repeatedly from above, and his prey had nary a chance. The second, a lion, based his claim on his strength—none dared to challenge him. The third, a skunk, insisted he needed neither flight nor strength to frighten off any creature. As the trio debated the issue, a grizzly bear came along and swallowed them all: hawk, lion, and *stinker!*" The speaker continues: The proposal sounds good, but the person making the presentation is glib! The facts will show we should not adopt it. Let's not fall hook, line and sinker or *stinker.*"

Burlesque.   This special form of exaggeration treats something absurd as though it is serious. For example:

A football coach named Bill tells his audience just how tenuous tenure is for football coaches at schools that take winning seriously. Coach Bill recounts how as a younger man he took a coaching position at a small eastern school. His predecessor had been fired for not winning enough games. "Still," Bill says, "There were no hard feelings between the two of us. In fact," Bill continues, "as Coach Stan cleaned out his desk, he said, 'I'm leaving two sealed envelopes for you in this top drawer. If early next year things aren't going well, open the first envelope. Inside are instructions that will tell you what to do. Then, if later on things still aren't going well, open the second envelope. Again, there are instructions that tell you what to do.'"

Coach Bill continues, "Well, we lost our first three games, so I decided to open the first envelope. Inside were the instructions: 'Blame everything on me. [signed] Stan.' So I told the alumni it was Stan's fault for leaving me a mess, but I would get it straightened out before our *must win* game with the Eagles late in the season. But we didn't do well all season, and we lost that big one to the Eagles. It was time to open that second envelope. So late Saturday night after the game, I went back to my office. I sat and thought for a while, and then I opened the drawer and looked at that second envelope. Finally, I opened it slowly and unfolded the letter inside. It said, 'Prepare two letters.'"

Capitalize on the rule of three.   Many good stories have three characters: a priest, a rabbi, and a minister; a blonde, a brunette, and a redhead; a soldier, a sailor, and a marine; Papa Bear, Momma Bear, and Baby Bear; an engineer, an accountant, and a teacher. Or a character behaves predictably the second time, but not the third. Remember the story of the duck earlier in this chapter? The first two requests for popcorn prepared the reader to expect the request again. But the duck asked a different question the third time.

Poke Fun at Yourself

Beware of poking fun at audience members, which may alienate your audience. Experienced speakers are careful in using humor at the expense of others. After time, speakers learn when it might be appropriate to poke fun at others. For example, Minnesotans and Iowans have much fun telling jokes at the expense of each other. But the humor is generic and not personal, and it's effective because of mutual respect. Even then, some hotheads take offense. So be careful. If you are not sure whether to use someone else as the butt of your humor, don't. But humor at your own expense is a different matter. People like to hear speakers poke fun at themselves.

Know the Audience

Chapter 1 devoted an entire section to knowing about your audience and told how a well-known comedian adjusted his use of humor to fit the audience. Knowing the audience is especially important when using humor. First, audiences turn off to speakers who attempt to use humor and fail. Second, humor is very tied to culture. What's funny in one part of the country or with a certain age group may not be funny in another part of the country or with a different age group.

Ensure Propriety

This point follows naturally from the previous one. Audiences differ. What might be appropriate for one audience may be inappropriate for another. Simply put, don't use inappropriate humor. If you don't know if a particular piece of humor is appropriate, treat it as though it isn't. Don't use it. Some speakers consider off-color stories or ethnic humor a cheap way to get a laugh from an audience. However, even people who laugh at such stories in private often lose respect for the speaker who uses them in public.

See Humor in the Situation

The best opportunity for adding humor may come in those minutes just before you speak. It may come from things said by those preceding you on the program. It may come from malfunction of your visual aids, from getting tangled up in the microphone cord, or from a person sneezing in your audience. And although much of this situational humor may not directly support the point you are making, it can nevertheless help win your audience.

Exercise   Poking Fun at Yourself

Make a list of things you can use to poke fun at yourself without hurting your credibility. You could use your state of residence: "I grew up in Kentucky; that probably explains a lot." "I'm a Texas Aggie, Auburn alum, Green Bay cheese head, Louisiana Cajun, etc." (take your pick). As you noticed, these are things their possessors are probably proud of. They are examples of positive ways to poke fun at oneself. Also consider physical characteristics. Your height—are you vertically challenged? The color of your hair, or your lack of hair—bald jokes are funniest when told by bald people. Stupid things you've done, such as dishing your food directly onto your tray without first putting a plate on the tray or locking your key in the car after your wife warned you that you should wire an extra one behind the bumper. You won't have to think very long in order to come up with quite a list, unless you are perfect or lack a sense of humor.

Exercise   Developing Your Own Repertoire of Humor

If you are serious about developing your own repertoire or collection of humor to use in presentations, this exercise will get you started. Create your own file. You can do this with a traditional file cabinet and file folders with headings that make sense to you, but a computerized file is best. I have more than 100 categories, including such topics as attitude, perseverance, workplace humor, marriage, focus, vision, and optimism. The point is that you determine the categories; they are yours. Put a good illustration or piece of humor into more than one folder. Of course, if you forget where you filed it electronically, go to the search function and enter a few words of the story and your computer should locate it for you.

Each time you hear good humor, write it down. Revise it. Adapt it to your style. Practice it with different people until you get the response you want. The more you use it, the more natural it will become. Copy and save good stories people send you through e-mail. Also use the common computer search engines—Google.com, Yahoo.com, and such—to locate literally millions of joke sites. Find ones that provide your style of humor. When you find a good story, copy it and put it in your file. A word of caution: most of the stuff you'll find is probably not worth using. Don't save it unless you believe you can use it in a future presentation.

Here are some things to keep in mind:

- Collect stories, illustrations, and other humor regularly.

- Don't trust your memory; write it down and get it in your files as soon as possible.

- Review your files from time to time so you will remember what you have.

- Back up your story files often—as you should with any important documents.

- If electronic, carry your files on a disk or CD when you travel. That way, you'll never be caught without them.

- Once you find a good source on the Internet, keep it in your list of favorites. Here are a few of mine: www.rd.com (*Reader's Digest*); http://FunnyCleanJokes.com (subscribe to this one free; it comes five days a week); http://humorlinks.com; and http://dmoz.org/Recreation/ Humor/. Just use one of the search engines and ask for "clean jokes," "college humor," "redneck jokes," or whatever you want. But cull it judiciously. And if you wonder if it is appropriate, it probably isn't.

Being witty and humorous takes effort. It helps to have an agile and sophisticated mind—one that adapts skillfully to the audience. Yet the skill of using humor can be learned and cultivated by almost anyone. Most speakers could use humor effectively if they were willing to practice. It is worth the effort because humorous support used effectively regains attention, builds rapport, enhances speaker credibility, aids retention, and improves listening—all highly desirable benefits.

Check Yourself: What Have You Learned?

☐ Humor regains attention, builds rapport, enhances speaker credibility, aids retention, and improves listening.

☐ Humor may be found in definitions, examples, comparisons, testimony, and statistics.

☐ To use humor effectively:

- Set it up.

- Time it.

- Vitalize it.

- Know the item thoroughly.

- Don't laugh before the audience does.

- Play on the unexpected.

- Poke fun at yourself.

- Know the audience.

- Make sure it's appropriate.

- See humor in the situation.

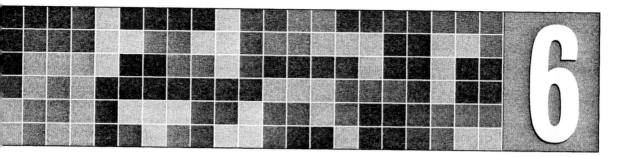

Using Visual Support

OBJECTIVE

- To comprehend how to use visual support in a presentation

TASKS

- Discuss various types of visual supporting materials, and tell how to use each type effectively.
- Explain the general guidelines for using visuals.

Verbal support is certainly at the heart of any good talk, but visual materials can also offer support. Often, visual aids work hand in hand with verbal support to dramatize, amplify, or clarify the points you want to get across to your audience. At other times, they function simply as an aid by listing points or subpoints you wish to cover. At still other times, visuals may function as stand-alone support; for this reason, this chapter treats visuals as supporting material.

This chapter does not focus on how to make fancy PowerPoint visuals, slides, posters, or charts. There is plenty of help for that on the Internet or through tutorials. Furthermore, great visual aids or visual support will not take the place of good content and strong delivery; in fact, they may detract by taking attention away from what the speaker is saying. This chapter focuses on how to use visuals as aids and as support.

INSIGHT	*Great visuals don't take the place of good content and strong delivery.*

WHY VISUALS ARE EFFECTIVE

When used well, visuals effectively assist the speaker, communicate information, and help the audience in at least four ways.

Visuals Gain Attention

People look at visuals; it's tough not to do so. We are a highly visual society. The next time you listen to a speech that uses visuals, notice where you look. It's automatic. Unless you are highly unusual, you will look at the visuals. Therefore, effective visuals can be a real asset in grabbing audience attention and directing it toward points the speaker wants to make.

Visuals Focus Thought

Either as an aid or as support for a point, visuals guide the audience's thinking. Visual *support* functions in the same way as verbal support by holding the listeners' attention and helping them understand, remember, and accept what is said. Visual *aids* clarify or explain what the speaker is saying. As aids or support, effective visuals focus audience thought.

Visuals Illustrate a Sequence

A visual that lists the main points of a speech shows listeners the order of the speaker's presentation. A visual showing the steps of a process helps listeners understand the order of the steps. If I were speaking to you about why visuals are effective, I might list the four points on a slide or chart— (1) gain attention, (2) focus thought, (3) illustrate a sequence, and (4) enhance remembering. The slide or chart would visually illustrate my order, or sequence, for you, my listener.

Visuals Enhance Remembering

People remember more of what they see than what they hear. Researchers tell us that people remember 10 percent of what they read, 20 percent of what they hear, 30 percent of what they see, and 50 percent of what they both hear and see. This is reason enough to use visuals when giving a presentation.

"The eye's a better pupil and more willing than the ear."

—Edgar A. Guest

KINDS OF VISUALS

The medium—the kind of visual—should suit the situation. PowerPoint presentations have become the standard medium in many places, but they are not the only way or necessarily the best way. At times, overhead transparencies, flipcharts, or even chalkboards may work better. They are often more available, simpler to use, require little or no setup, and lack the rigidity or straitjacket effect of "canned" PowerPoint presentations. Different kinds of visuals have different advantages and disadvantages for the speaker.

"Dr Gus moved across the front of the room, talking a mile a minute, chalk in one hand, following up with the eraser in the other. It was chalk dust in motion."

—former student remembering a professor

Chalkboard or Whiteboard

For over 100 years, chalkboards were a mainstay. In fact, for many people, the term *visual aid* meant chalkboard. Then yesterday's chalkboard—usually black with white chalk—became today's whiteboard with a variety of colored markers. Colored markers allow speakers to depict parts of a diagram or highlight various points. Both chalkboards and whiteboards have the advantages of being inexpensive, simple to use, and highly adaptable since changes can be made on the spot. On the other hand, they are not novel and therefore don't command as much attention as some other media. Furthermore, they present a distinct disadvantage in that speakers must turn their backs on audiences to use them. If you use a chalkboard or whiteboard, consider these suggestions:

- On a whiteboard, use markers that make a broad enough iine to be seen. For chalkboards, pare chalk to the desired thickness so that the lines you draw are 1/4 to 3/8 inch wide. Have spare markers and chalk ready for use.

- Use colors of markers or chalk that make a sharp contrast with the board and can be easily seen by the audience.

- On whiteboards, use washable markers rather than permanent ones if you plan to use the board again.

- Consider using a No. 2 soft pencil and yardstick to make erasable guidelines on the board before your audience enters the room. Later, when writing on the board during your talk, you can ensure straight and even lettering by following lines invisible to your audience. This works especially well on black chalkboards.

- Cramping your letters and diagrams cramps your speaking. To be seen easily at 30 feet, letters should be about 3 inches high.

- Avoid using the bottom half of the board if you are speaking from the same floor level as your audience, since some listeners may be unable to see.

- Determine where glare on the board is a distraction. Before the audience enters the room, adjust window blinds or avoid these areas of the board.

- If the room is equipped with a magnetic chalkboard, or if some other metal surface such as a file cabinet is nearby, consider preconstructed visual aids with magnets glued to the back. Reusable magnetic material one inch wide can be purchased in long lengths and cut easily to the desired length. Two magnets, each one inch square, will support one square foot of lightweight illustration board.

INSIGHT	*If I can't see it, I can't understand it.*

Flipcharts

After the arrival of felt-tip markers, but before the advent of today's high-tech age, flipcharts grew in popularity. They have been especially popular with teachers or speakers who find it necessary to move from room to room and repeat a presentation. The board doesn't need to be erased; the visuals don't have to be redrawn. And flipcharts have the advantages of being inexpensive and easy to make, either freehand or by using mechanical lettering templates. Although technology has in many cases passed them by, flipcharts still have their place and, like chalkboards and whiteboards, they are highly adaptable since speakers can write as they speak—although having one's back to the audience can still pose a problem. Here are some suggestions for using flipcharts:

- *Keep them simple.*   The visual should aid or support the presentation. Too much writing or drawing on a chart is likely to confuse rather than help listeners.

- *Use bold lines.*   Bold lines are easier to see, and bold letters are easier to read. Make it easy on your listeners.

- *Be clear.*   Clarity of letters, optical spacing, and appropriate lettering style are important because flipcharts must be legible from a distance.

- *Consider separating individual sheets.*   Clip them to an easel with large black paper clips to give you the flexibility to change the order of presentation.

- *Avoid the use of permanent markers.*   They may bleed through the paper onto other pages.

- *Back up the flipchart with additional sheets of paper.*   Flipchart paper is normally translucent, allowing information on the next chart to be visible from the chart on top. Even better, to conserve paper, save time, and look like a pro, reverse the process and *flip the charts from rear to front.* It's also easier to flip the charts this way than to flip them over the easel from front to rear—and you're less likely to knock over the easel.

"The paper hung up on top of the easel, I gave an extra push and it collapsed. I had trouble regaining my composure."

                        —a student explaining what happened while using flipcharts

INSIGHT

A small portable *briefaid* (see Figure 6.1) is a handy variant of the larger flipchart. Useful for small groups, it can be set up on a desk in front of you or, if you're standing behind a lectern, you can hang it over the edge. In either position, you can maintain eye contact with your audience and still have good control over your visuals. All you need is a hardcover three-ring binder, clear plastic document protectors, and 8 1/2-by-11 inch sheets of paper. Furthermore, notes that accompany the slide can be placed on the back of the next page—available to you when you need them, but out of sight to the audience when you flip the page.

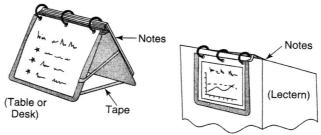

FIGURE 6.1   Notes displayed on a briefaid.

Exercise   Making and Using Flipcharts

Construct a five-page flipchart presentation (or use a portable briefaid). The first sheet should say "Why Visuals Are Effective." Each of the following four pages should give one of the reasons listed at the beginning of this chapter: gain attention, focus thought, illustrate a sequence, and enhance remembering. Make the letters large and bold enough to be seen. Practice flipping them as described earlier from rear to front while presenting a mini-talk using the information contained in the section at the beginning of this chapter titled "Why Visuals Are Effective."

Posters or Charts

Posters or charts are often used to emphasize a theme or present some piece of information visually. Pie charts, graphs, and tables may appear on posters, especially when speakers want to point out different aspects of the poster or even display the poster or chart throughout the presentation. For example, a United Way campaign chairperson used a chart with a drawing of a large thermometer. The top of the thermometer represented the campaign goal. The bottom half was painted red, showing that half of the money toward the goal had been pledged. The chairperson used a pie chart to show how each sector—education, residential, corporations, professions, and so forth—was doing.

INSIGHT   *It's true that a picture is worth a thousand words—but only if it is well done.*

Maps, bar graphs, pie charts, line graphs, and picture graphs can all serve not only as outstanding visual aids but also as visual support for the points a speaker wants to make. Posters and charts can be extremely useful, but consider several things:

- Artistry does not substitute for content.
- Fancy posters take time. Ask yourself: "Is it worth it?"
- The poster should not rely on your verbal explanation to link together the various portions.
- If you have about 20 percent text, 40 percent graphics, and 40 percent empty space, you are doing well.
- Use active voice when writing the text; for example, say, "The data show . . ." instead of "It can be seen . . ."
- Remove all material extraneous to the focal point of the poster.

- There's almost *always* too much text in a poster, so edit ruthlessly!
- Make certain everyone can see the poster.

"Nice posters. Wish they made sense."   **INSIGHT**

—CEO of a large company after listening to a presentation

Exercise   Using Posters

Give an impromptu talk using a poster supplied by your teacher or trainer. Discuss the poster, and point out various parts of it. The purpose is to make certain you use the visual aid appropriately, looking at the audience as much as possible and not obstructing their view of the poster. This is not a "show-and-tell" performance but a talk on a subject for which the visual is not only a convenience but a necessity.

Overhead Transparencies

These old standbys, often referred to simply as "overheads," offer definite advantages. First, you can see your transparencies on the projector and still maintain good eye contact with the audience. Second, you are not locked into a certain sequence and can make changes in the order or choose not to show a given transparency if the situation arises. Third, unlike many other projectors, you can leave the lights on and still see the image on the screen. Finally, you can make inexpensive, professional-looking transparencies with your computer and printer using inexpensive transparency film or acetate sheets available in office supply stores. Consider the following points when using overheads:

- Keep visuals simple. Avoid clutter.
- Never project a full page of typewritten material. It's too much to read and too small to see.
- Use a typesize large enough to be seen—usually 28 point or larger depending on the size of the screen and the distance of the projector from the screen. (The next section on PowerPoint discusses more about type size or font size and style.)
- When not showing a transparency, either turn the projector off or attach a small piece of cardboard with masking tape so it hangs down in front of the lens when you don't want to project an image and can be flipped back when you do. This keeps light from projecting on the screen or wall when the projector is not showing an image.

FIGURE 6.2   Avoid distortion by properly aligning the projector.

- Align the projector so the image shows directly on the screen. If the projector is not square with the wall, the image will appear longer on one side than the other. If the image is projected upward, a *keystone effect* will result (as seen in Figure 6.2).
- Put individual transparencies in cardboard frames obtained from an office supply store to make them appear more professional and to make handling easier.
- Write notes or reminders on the cardboard frames. By all means number them; then, if they get out of order, you can reorder them quickly.
- Reveal one line at a time by blocking out text below with a sheet of paper. Simply slide the paper down to reveal the next point when you are ready to talk about it. This keeps listeners' attention focused on the point you are discussing. Best results come from placing the paper under the transparency against the glass. When placed on top of the transparency, the paper tends to shift.
- Make slides colorful by using a color printer, colored acetate sheets, or even different-colored markers to highlight points.

INSIGHT   *"I dropped all 65 transparencies. It took five minutes to get them back in order. I wish I'd numbered them."*

—Army major telling about his experience of briefing his commander

PowerPoint

This most popular of all computer-generated graphics has become the expectation of many audiences, especially in corporate America and also in the military and other federal agencies. Such computer-generated graphics allow the development and display of words, charts, graphs, and pictures, as well as the integration of sound and videos or DVDs into presentations. Although you may either know how to use PowerPoint and much of the associated technology or have friends who can help you, having technology "know-how" is no guarantee that you know how to design and present high-tech visuals. In fact, high technical literacy can be a hindrance, for such persons often want to use the available technology for its own sake rather than to communicate—that is, to aid understanding or support points being made.

PowerPoint used well is a tremendous tool. But there is an art to developing effective PowerPoint presentations and an art to using them.

"Just because PowerPoint lets you do it doesn't mean you should." **INSIGHT**

—Teri Henley, professor of advertising, Loyola University of New Orleans, and coach of National Championship Advertising Teams

Some of the following guidelines for using PowerPoint also apply to the media discussed previously—chalkboards, whiteboards, flipcharts, posters, charts, and overheads. Some also restate or touch on suggestions or considerations raised earlier.

Simplify.   Too many speakers write too much text on the slides. Replace sentences with key words and phrases. Generally, use punctuation only if absolutely needed. Don't fall into the trap of using fancy fonts, images, clip art, and sounds, which usually detract from your message. Visuals should support or aid in presenting your message.

Follow the "triple 6" rule.   That is, after the heading, use no more than six lines and no more than six words to a line. Also, the audience should grasp the slide's meaning in six seconds. Have good reasons for exceptions to this rule. For example, in listing the names of the supporting characters from the story "Snow White and the Seven Dwarfs," which one would you leave out? Dopey, Sneezy, Doc? In this case, you would make an exception and keep them all.

Consider using "build-up slides."   When there's too much information for viewers to grasp in six seconds, or if you want to focus audience attention on each point as you discuss it, use build-up slides. Build-up slides, on which each point appears as you click, give the same effect as using a piece of paper to cover and then reveal points on an overhead, with a notable exception—with PowerPoint, you can make the previous point fade or disappear when the new one appears. In any case, have each new point "appear" rather than "fly," "crawl," or "peek." It's more professional and less distracting.

Choose your typeface carefully.   New and exciting font styles appear often. Have fun experimenting, but don't go crazy. Some advocates contend that serif fonts, such as the ones used in this book, are easier to read because the little lines at the top and bottom of the letters—serifs—help guide the eye from letter to letter. Sans serif fonts (fonts without serifs) don't do this. This contention may be true for the printed word where the reader is dealing with large blocks of copy, but actually sans serif fonts give a cleaner, less cluttered effect on slides. Do choose a font that is easy to read. Avoid script, decorative fonts, and italics except to highlight certain words or communicate a certain tone or mood.

You may use **boldface** type for PowerPoint slides, unless it makes the type look "fat" or rounded and difficult to read. This is often the case. Experiment to find out what works best.

Use both capital and lowercase letters.   It is easier for your audience to read mixed cases. Don't shout at viewers with all caps.

USING BOTH LOWER- AND UPPERCASE
LETTERS MAKES A SLIDE EASIER TO
READ, TAKES UP LESS SPACE, AND
DOESN'T SHOUT AT LISTENERS.

Using both lower- and uppercase letters
makes a slide easier to read, takes up less
space, and doesn't shout at listeners.

Be consistent on font use.   First, within a slide—you may use more than one typeface or font on a slide, but using more than two tends to clutter the visual and confuse the audience. Second, between and among slides—jumping from typeface to typeface or format to format detracts from professionalism and hinders communication.

Be consistent with backgrounds.   I am constantly amazed at how many people "mix it up" to keep things interesting. Actually, varying backgrounds distracts the audience.

Be consistent with transitions.   Just because PowerPoint lets you do random ones doesn't mean you should.

Build in gaps with neutral slides. Neutral slides allow you to talk to the audience with no visual showing. Or, if you are controlling your own slides from a laptop, simply press the letter *b* for the screen to go black or *w* for the screen to go white. Press the letter again, and the slide reappears. A period also works. Also, have a neutral slide at the end, or perhaps end the presentation with a visual identical to the opening one, with the presentation title, the name of presenter, and whatever else is appropriate.

Use color to attract, highlight, contrast, or create a feeling or mood. Some research indicates that using color increases willingness to read the visual, retention of the material, and acceptance of an idea. Furthermore, the evidence is clear that color outsells black and white. But keep in mind the following points about color.

- Bright colors are easier to see than pastels.
- Use of too many colors can give a confused and cluttered effect.
- Multiple colors are useful for many charts, graphs, maps, and such.
- Use light (white or yellow, for example) letters on a dark background or dark letters on a light background. This contrast is needed. For example, black letters are difficult to see on a dark blue or black background.
- A light background will keep the room lighter, but light letters (such as white or yellow on a dark blue or black background) are easy to read, as are some other combinations. Aim for easier readability.
- Some people experience color insensitivity. Most common is reduced sensitivity to reds and greens—about 10 percent of men experience this "color blindness." If you put red letters on a green background, 10 percent of the men in your audience won't be able to read your slides.
- Be aware that the colors you see on your computer screen may project somewhat differently on a screen or in a large room. Try projecting your slides before you present them. Besides, it's always a good idea to do a dry run of your presentation, if possible in the room where you will be speaking.
- If you are projecting your own slides, be very familiar with the computer you are using. If someone else is projecting them, talk with him to make certain he understands any special needs you have.
- If you are attaching your computer to a projector you haven't used before, make sure you have connectivity. Learn how to use the appropriate function (F) keys to make your computer and projector work together. *Don't take this advice lightly*—it comes from the voice of experience!

■ Before your presentation, make sure you cover the lens of the projector while you are setting up, so the PowerPoint architecture doesn't show on the screen.

INSIGHT	*"Cover your lens during setup so your PowerPoint underwear doesn't show."* —Teri Henley

■ Make certain the fonts you used when designing your slides are available on the computer you will be using. If the fonts aren't available, your slides will be distorted. While this is not usually a problem with PCs, it's a good idea with Macintoshes to download your font on a disk or CD.
■ Use sound effects sparingly, if at all. Use them only if you have a good reason. There are few good reasons, one of which might be to focus attention, and another, to add variety.
■ If you have your presentation on a floppy disk, don't fasten it to your refrigerator with a magnet so you won't forget to take it with you. Magnets ruin the data. Again, *don't take this advice lightly.*

INSIGHT	*"PowerPoint gives you all the tools you need to make a truly tacky presentation."* —Teri Henley

Exercise   Making and Using PowerPoint Slides

If you have access to PowerPoint capability, use the following information to construct a four-slide PowerPoint presentation on "The Importance of Visuals." We spend 50 percent of our communication time listening, 25 percent speaking, 15 percent reading, and 10 percent writing. Researchers tell us people remember 10 percent of what they read, 20 percent of what they hear, 30 percent of what they see, and 50 percent of what they both hear and see. This is reason enough to use visuals when giving a presentation—more specifically, visuals hold attention, focus thought, illustrate a sequence or list, and enhance remembering.

The first slide should be a title slide—"The Importance of Visuals"; the other three will be content slides. Review the suggestions given on making PowerPoint slides. For an additional challenge, prepare a mini-lecture to accompany the slides. Remember, don't simply read the slides.

Videotapes and Movies

Many classrooms, training rooms, and other places people speak have easy access to videotape players and monitors. Used judiciously, videos and movies can provide outstanding visual support for a point you want to make. For example, I recently conducted several hours of training on "Meeting the Media." My audience needed to know how to handle interviews with the press and television. I used segments from interviews taped off the air to illustrate good and bad techniques of interviewing. I also showed a five-minute segment from a television sitcom that humorously illustrated several points I wished to make. Finally, I previously videotaped short segments with two actors to illustrate various techniques I wished to teach. Videos and movies offer obvious advantages and opportunities for presenting supporting material, but keep several things in mind:

- Whereas a 25-inch monitor is generally large enough for 25 people, you'll need additional monitors or a larger screen for larger audiences.

- Although videos and movies can be dramatic and capture attention, ask yourself whether they will add or detract from your speech. Sometimes the "star" quality of the actors and actresses overshadows your speech. Also, movie segments were not made as stand-alone packages but as part of a larger story.

- When you make your own videos, you have absolute control over the content, but your videos may lack professional quality and cast a bad light on your speech. Also, the process of making your own videos is time-consuming. Ask yourself if it's worth the time.

- When showing videos or movies, be sure you know the equipment you will be using and have videotapes and movies "keyed" and ready to go to avoid undesirable pauses during your presentation.

Audiotapes

Strictly speaking, audio aids are not visuals, but don't overlook their value. An old standby, a cassette recorder, can be a great asset for speakers. For a speech on a newly proposed tax, a speaker interviews people, selects segments, and plays them as support material in her speech. At times, rather than read a quotation, I say, "Let's see what Colin Powell said about that." Then, rather than quote Powell, I play a taped segment of him speaking. Or I say, "Let's see what Abraham Lincoln said." Obviously, I don't have a tape of Lincoln speaking, so I play a recording of someone reading the words as Lincoln might have said them. Playing a tape—even one of someone else reading Lincoln's words—lends authenticity. Also, it gives the speaker a chance to rest her voice and collect her thoughts. If using a microphone, simply hold the cassette player close to it so the sound goes through the sound system. You may wish to put recordings on CD-ROMs or even floppy disks rather than using audiocassettes.

CD-ROMs and DVDs

Popular compact disks and digital videodisks provide great opportunities to speakers. Most computers now have CD-ROM drives. This ability to store and process information digitally allows one disk to store hundreds of images, multiple audio recordings, and massive amounts of information, even an entire encyclopedia. And it's available at your fingertips. You can store PowerPoint slides, movie clips, and recordings on one CD and use them all to support points you make in a speech.

DVDs look and operate like CDs but contain much more information. A whole movie can be stored on a DVD, and the picture quality is much better. In fact, it is superb. And since a DVD can, like a videocassette recorder, be connected directly to a television set and also to a computer, the opportunity to use a DVD to handle support material is outstanding. Furthermore, the capability to start and stop a DVD at a precise spot makes DVDs well suited for integration into a speech or other presentation.

Props

Prop is simply a shortened version of *property*, a word used to describe any object used in a theatrical performance. Speakers, like actors, are performers. (This fact will become evident in Chapter 9, which focuses on delivery.) Speakers also share with actors the obligation to use whatever is necessary to get their points across to an audience. The lectern you stand behind, and the flipcharts, markers, slides, recorders, notes, posters, charts, and in fact all the items you use, are props. Items you display before, during, or after the speech are props.

> A motivational speaker holds up a key ring with several keys and says, "Today I want to talk with you about the keys to success." A teacher holds up a large picture of Martin Luther King Jr. and asks, "How many of you know who this man is?" An Air Force pilot says, "I fly the KC-135 tanker." At this point, he pulls the cover off a model of the aircraft and says, "To many of you, this may look a lot like the Boeing 707 that you have flown on many times. It is the same airframe, but there are some real differences—differences that make it a real workhorse. We couldn't win our wars without the KC-135."

These three speakers—the motivational speaker, the teacher, and the pilot—used props effectively. The speaker's key ring focuses audience attention on her subject, the keys to success; the teacher has the students' attention as he talks about the contributions of Martin Luther King Jr.; and the pilot has the attention of the civic club as he tells about the plane and the missions he has flown.

During a lesson on visual supporting material, a teacher holds up a DVD in one hand and an old-style 78RPM record in another and says there are similarities. Both are disks, but that's about all these two objects have in common. She then proceeds to tell how much information could be stored on each disk. Not only has she used a graphic comparison between the two props, but she has clearly shown what a DVD looks like. If her students didn't already know, they do now—and they won't forget. Such is the value of props. Here are a few tips to keep in mind:

- When size allows, keep special props hidden until you are ready to use them, and then hide them again when finished; otherwise, listeners may continue to focus on them.
- Make certain the prop is large enough to be seen by all of the audience. We've all seen speakers hold up a small photograph and say, "You probably can't see this in the back of the room, but it shows my visit to the pyramids of Egypt." The speaker should have left the photo at home. If the audience can't see it or make sense out of it, don't use it.
- Don't pass the prop around. Everyone will not be able to see it at the appropriate time, and you will lose the attention of the listener who is looking at it at that time.
- Always speak to the audience, not the prop.
- Make certain the audience is ready to focus on the prop, especially if the prop is supposed to have a surprise effect.
- As with all visuals, use props only if they aid communication or support a point.

Exercise   Practice Using Props

Your trainer or teacher will have a box full of objects and will hand one of the objects to a participant, asking him or her to immediately present an informal talk using the object either as a visual aid or as visual support for the point to be made. A variation: Your teacher or trainer will pick some object in the room—a picture, piece of chalk, book, soda can, book bag—hand it to the participant, and tell him or her to give a two-minute talk on the object. Follow the tips given on using props.

GUIDELINES FOR USING VISUALS

By now, it's clear that all visual methods—chalkboards, whiteboards, flipcharts, posters, charts, overheads, PowerPoint slides, videotapes, movies, CDs, DVDs, and props of all types—share one thing in common: they appeal to the sense of sight. It's also clear that many of the suggestions, considerations, tips, and guidelines given for a certain medium also apply to other ones. Some of the points made earlier need reemphasis, however. Perhaps not all of the following guidelines apply to you. For instance, some apply to persons who travel to make presentations at another site but may not apply to students giving presentations in a classroom. Still, the following 14 points provide a good checklist to review before using visuals in your speech.

Use only relevant materials.   Avoid using materials solely for aesthetic or interest value. Certainly, visual materials should be interesting and aesthetically pleasing, but use visuals either to support a point or to aid understanding.

Make visuals large enough to be seen.   Ensure that all visual materials are large enough to be seen by the entire audience. It's disturbing to be seated in the back of the room and unable to see the visuals. In preparing for your talk, display the visual and then move yourself to the location of your most distant listener. If you can't readily see the material, don't use it.

Keep visuals simple and clear.   Emphasize only the most important information. Omit unnecessary details. A series of simple charts is preferable to a single complicated one. Remember that the briefing, lecture, or speech is the primary means of communication. Visuals simply provide support or serve as aids to the talk.

Use visuals only at the proper time.   Don't pass visuals around for the audience to handle and view during your speech. This steals the listeners' attention from you. Also, don't expose the visual material until the proper point in the talk. Materials that are visible too soon or that remain in view after the point has been made distract and interrupt the continuity of the talk. Put props out of sight, cover flipcharts, erase whiteboards, use build-up slides—do what is necessary to keep visuals out of view at inappropriate times.

Talk to the audience, not to your visuals.   If you are explaining a chart or prop, look at your audience as much as possible. By the time you make your talk, be familiar with your visuals so you won't need to look at them closely.

Don't read from the visual.   Especially if the visual is functioning as an aid, avoid reading from it. Pause; allow the audience to read it for themselves. Or, if you talk as you show a slide or other visual, paraphrase what's on the visual.

Place visuals away from obstructions.   Don't allow other projects or persons, including yourself, to obstruct your audience's view of the visual. This hinders the effectiveness of the visuals.

Check your equipment beforehand. If you plan to use equipment, such as an overhead projector, a slide projector, or a film projector, make certain beforehand that you know how to use the equipment and that it is set up and ready to go. Also, know whether or not you have spare bulbs, how to change them, or how to improvise. In other words, be ready for any contingencies that may develop. Many potentially sound presentations fail because the speaker has not planned for equipment that malfunctions.

Proofread visuals carefully. Then get someone else to proof them. Do not depend on spell check; it won't catch everything. Typos, misprints, misspelled words—these and other errors call attention to themselves and hurt your credibility and the effectiveness of the presentation.

Carry backup material for your presentation. For instance, I often e-mail PowerPoint slides ahead of time to the place of the presentation, but I always carry all the material backed up on either a floppy disk or a CD. This practice also allows me to have all my backup material, references, and anything else I might need. Also, if the presentation is important, consider making overhead transparencies or having material available on a handout just in case. Having one hard copy (photocopy) of the slides allows for quick copying and distribution.

> *"The likelihood equipment won't work is inversely proportional to the importance of the presentation."*
>
> —Teri Henley

INSIGHT

Practice, practice, practice using your visuals. At first, it may seem that visuals make things easier because they can act as a crutch or memory jogger. But visuals are one more thing to be concerned about as you attempt to integrate them into the presentation at just the right time. If possible, practice in the room and with the equipment where you will make the presentation.

Get there early. When you are rushed, more bad things are apt to happen. Early arrival allows you to take care of personal needs, check the equipment, go over your notes, and think things through. It also allows you time to rearrange the room or equipment to ensure that you make the best presentation possible. Of course, rearrangement is not always possible, but at least you will have time to adapt to the setting.

Keep your visuals with you. If you are traveling by air, carry them rather than checking them through. I once left my notes and overheads tucked under the lectern so I would have them when I went to speak. I left the room for a few minutes. While I was gone, workers replaced the lectern with another, but they didn't leave my transparencies or my notes. Again, *don't take this advice lightly*.

Make sure the time and expense are justified.   Ask yourself if the time and expense required to prepare or procure the visuals are justified and add significantly to the overall value of the talk. If not, forget it. Often the time spent preparing visuals could be better spent preparing and practicing the talk.

INSIGHT	*"Think of visuals as accessories. Too much looks tacky; too little, and it's not together. The right accessories make the outfit."*
	—Teri Henley

Check Yourself: What Have You Learned?

☐ Visuals don't take the place of good content and strong delivery.

☐ Visuals can gain attention, focus thought, illustrate a sequence, and enhance remembering.

☐ Visuals should suit the situation.

☐ Guidelines should be followed when using each kind of visual: chalkboards or whiteboards, flipcharts, posters or charts, overhead transparencies, PowerPoint slides, videotapes and movies, audiotapes, CD-ROMs and DVDs, and props.

☐ General guidelines for using visuals include the following:

- Use only relevant materials.
- Make them large enough to be seen.
- Keep them simple and clear.
- Use them only at the proper time.
- Talk to the audience, not the visual.
- Don't read from the visual.
- Place visuals away from obstructions.
- Make certain you can run the equipment.
- Proofread visuals carefully.
- Carry backup material for your presentation.
- Carry copies of all visuals on CD.
- Practice, practice, practice.
- Get there early.
- Keep visuals with you.
- Make certain the time and expense of visuals are justified.

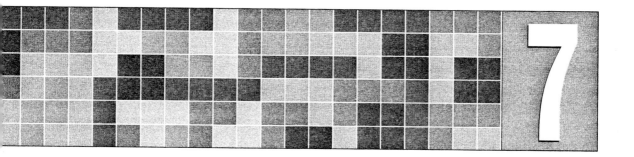

Beginnings, Endings, and Transitions

OBJECTIVE

- To comprehend how to begin presentations, end presentations, and transition between parts of presentations

TASKS

- Demonstrate how to begin and end different types of presentations.
- Give examples of appropriate ways to gain attention at the beginning.
- Differentiate among the different kinds of transitions, and give examples of each.

Once you have organized and supported the body of your talk with appropriate verbal and visual materials, you must decide how to begin, end, and tie it all together with smooth transitions. For many persons, beginning (or providing an introduction to the body of the talk) and ending (providing a conclusion) are the most troublesome. Others have trouble preparing effective transitions between different parts of their presentations. This chapter tells how to begin and end different kinds of presentations, then focuses on how to gain attention at the beginning of a talk, and finally explains how to prepare effective transitions that add polish to the talk.

BEGINNING AND ENDING VARIOUS TYPES OF TALKS

Beginnings and endings should fit the audience, the speaker, and the type of talk you are giving. In Chapter 1, I said that the generic title *speech* is often used to refer to three major types of talks—briefings, lectures, and speeches. In following chapters, I mentioned that certain kinds of supporting materials are more suited for some types of talks than others. You will also want to prepare different kinds of beginnings and endings for each type of talk. Recall that briefings present information quickly and concisely, lectures are used to teach new material, and speeches are given in a variety of situations. There are different ways to begin and end talks, just as there are different ways to organize and support them.

INSIGHT	*Every speech needs a good beginning and a good ending, preferably close together.*

Briefings

Since briefings must be concise, lengthy beginnings and endings are inappropriate. Briefings are given to busy people who desire and need to know your information, so don't waste time on a long beginning or ending. A chief financial officer (CFO) briefing the CEO and vice presidents of a bank on its current financial status, a military officer briefing higher-ranking officers on a proposal to upgrade enlisted barracks on the base, and the chairperson of the United Way briefing sector chiefs on the progress of a campaign are all examples of briefings.

Beginning.   If, as often happens, another speaker introduces you and your subject, you may only need to give a quick overview of the subject and proceed immediately to the main points. Your listeners' familiarity with the subject will determine the length of the overview. In most cases, simply mentioning the main points is sufficient. If you are not introduced, you might simply say, "Good morning, I'm _____ briefing on _____. Here are the main points we will cover today." Often, just a couple of seconds before you begin speaking or at the moment you actually begin, you may show a PowerPoint slide, chart, or transparency with the title of your presentation, your name, and (if appropriate) the name of your company or organization on whose behalf you are speaking. You can use another visual listing your main points. Then get into the body of your talk. If you expect a decision from your listeners at the end of your talk, tell them at the beginning.

Ending.   This part of a briefing should be short but positive. Generally, you will end by reiterating the main points of the briefing, usually with an accompanying slide or chart showing the points. If you are recommending a particular solution or course of action, say so. Give a brief, clear restatement of the possible solution or course of action you judge best. No new material or commentary should be presented here. You have given the information in the body of the talk. Now conclude quickly. Briefings are to be brief.

Although many briefings are subject to interruption for questions from listeners, many times a good concluding sentence might be: "Ladies and Gentlemen, are there any (further) questions?" If a question period is not to follow, or once the questions have ended, you might simply say, "Ladies and Gentlemen, that concludes my briefing," or "Thank you for inviting me to speak to you today," or "Thank you, I look forward to talking more with you about this concept [proposal/idea]." Often, the highest-ranking person listening to your briefing or the person conducting the meeting may conclude the question period for you by declaring, for example, "We have no further questions." Depending on the situation, you will say either nothing or else a short "Thank you." Usually, briefings are one item on a longer agenda. Listeners will be ready to move to the next item.

Follow the ABCs of briefing—Accuracy, Brevity, Clarity.   **INSIGHT**

Lectures

Learning is generally the desired outcome of lectures. The beginning of a lecture prepares learners to listen. The ending helps them synthesize material presented in the lecture. Whether the lecture is presented live in front of a group of learners or through distance technology via CDs, DVDs, videotape, or live presentation on computer screens or large television screens at remote locations, effective beginnings and endings are important for lectures.

Beginning.   The beginning of a lecture serves several purposes: to establish a common ground between the speaker and the learners, to capture and hold attention, to outline the lecture and relate it to the overall course, to point out benefits to the listeners, and to lead into the lecture content. Although humor may be appropriate, the beginning should be free of irrelevant stories, jokes, or incidents that distract from the lesson objective, and it should not contain long or apologetic remarks that are likely to dampen student interest in the lesson. Educators often speak of three necessary elements in the introduction of a lecture: (1) gaining attention, (2) motivating, and (3) providing an overview of material to be covered in the lecture.

1. *Attention.*   You may tell a story that relates to the subject and provides a background for the lecture. Or, perhaps you'll want to use an appropriate quotation or humorous anecdote. Another technique is to make an unexpected or surprising statement or ask a question that relates the lecture to the group's needs. A closed or rhetorical question—one that does not expect an audible response (for example, Have you ever . . . ? or Can you imagine . . . ?)—might be effective. At other times, nothing more than a clear indication that the lecture has begun is sufficient. In all instances, the primary concern is to focus listener attention on the subject. Later, this chapter gives techniques for getting audience attention.

2. *Motivation.*   After you are sure listeners are paying attention, give specific reasons why they should listen. Tell why they need to learn or know what you plan to lecture about. You will recall from Chapter 1 that all speaking should be listener centered. This is why a motivational step is so important when lecturing. In this step, you make a personal appeal to listeners and reinforce their desire to learn. The appeal may relate learning to career advancement, financial gain, service to the community, use at home, or some other need, but in every instance, you should cite a specific application for what listeners will learn from the lecture. For example, in subjects such as mathematics, a certain concept must be learned before a student can use an important formula. In athletics, fundamentals must be mastered before one can compete successfully.

Of course, motivational appeals should continue throughout the lecture. If you briefly mention student needs only at the beginning, you fill the square but do not keep motivating your listeners to learn. Effective talks of all kinds—briefings, lectures, speeches—motivate listeners throughout the presentation.

"Most of the problems of education are problems of motivation. . . . Motivate the student and . . . the teacher cannot keep him from learning."

—Rousseau

3. *Overview.* The third step of the introduction or beginning is to provide an overview of what you plan to cover during the lecture. A clear, concise presentation of the objective and key ideas serves as a road map for learning. Effective visual aids can be helpful at this point. Suppose I am lecturing on "How to Begin and End a Lecture." After my attention and motivation steps I might show the visual that appears as Figure 7.1 and say, "So today we will learn how to begin and end lectures effectively. First, we will look at the three steps that ensure an effective beginning—how to gain attention, how to motivate the audience to listen, and how to provide an overview or a road map for what you plan to cover. Second, we will look at the three steps that will provide a good ending to the lecture—the summary, where you repeat the major points and help listeners tie things together; the remotivation, which emphasizes the importance of remembering and applying what they learned; and finally, the closure, which gives a sense of completeness and releases listeners from listening."

> *"I knew the church service was over when I finally heard the benediction."*
>
> —comment by a fourth grader

INSIGHT

A clear overview contributes greatly to a lecture by removing doubts in the minds of listeners about where the lesson is going and how they are going to get there. You can tell students what will be covered or left out and why. Here is where you tell them how the lecture is organized. Listeners understand better and retain more when they know what to expect. The purpose of the overview is to prepare students to listen to the body of the lecture.

Overview of a Talk on "How to Begin and End a Lecture"

- Beginning
  - Attention
  - Motivation
  - Overview
- Ending
  - Summary
  - Remotivation
  - Closure

FIGURE 7.1 *A sample overview.*

"Learning is a result of listening."

                                    —Alice Miller

Ending.   The conclusion of a lecture may stick with listeners longer than anything else said. For this reason, you should prepare it carefully. The conclusion of most lectures should accomplish three things: summarize, remotivate, and provide closure.

1. *Final summary.*   Mini- or interim summaries may be appropriate at various places in a lecture—for example, after each main point has been made. But final summaries come after you've made all your main points in the lecture. An effective final summary retraces the important elements discussed in the body of the talk. As the term suggests, a *final summary* concisely reviews the main points of the lecture. Reviewing main points can aid listeners' retention of information and give them a chance to fill in missing information in their minds and in their notes. Don't use the final summary to reteach material or go into each point in detail. Keep summaries as brief as possible. While presenting the summary, you may want to show the same slide you showed for the overview with the title changed to say "Summary." The slide will focus listeners' attention on what you are saying.

2. *Remotivation.*   The purpose of the remotivation is to instill in listeners a desire to retain and use what they have learned. Effective speakers provide motivation throughout the lecture, but the remotivation step is the instructor's last chance to let learners know why the information presented in the lecture is important to them. Perhaps the information is important because it provides groundwork for future lessons or because it will help them do their jobs more effectively. Whatever the reasons given, they should appeal directly to the listeners and show the importance to them of what was learned.

3. *Closure.*   Closure presents a difficult challenge for many speakers. Learners need to be released from listening, but the closure should communicate a feeling of completeness and leave listeners with a positive feeling. Sometimes, at a loss on how to close, instructors say, "Well, that's about all I have to say" or "I guess I don't have anything else." This type of closure is not very satisfying. There are much more effective ways of closing. Sometimes, vocal inflection can signal that the lecture is ending. Quotations, stories, or humorous incidents can also provide effective closure.

"The speaker was finished 20 minutes before he quit talking; that's when we quit listening."

                              —overheard on a college campus

Sometimes when the lecture is to be followed by other lessons in the same block of instruction, you might say something such as "Next time, then, we will continue with our discussion of _____. Between now and then, if you have any questions, call me, fax me, send me an e-mail, or come see me, and I'll see if I can answer them for you." Of course if you say this, make certain that listeners know your fax and phone numbers, your e-mail address, and where to find you. In all my lectures and especially in all training sessions I conduct, I give my numbers, e-mail address, and website on my first and last PowerPoint visual. I also often supply them on a written handout.

The beginning steps of attention, motivation, and overview and the ending steps of summary, remotivation, and closure are excellent ways to start and end a lecture. These steps are often appropriate for general speeches as well, but there are exceptions.

Speeches

All speeches need strong beginnings and endings, but the types of beginnings and endings needed may differ greatly from speech to speech.

"Tell them what you're going to tell them; tell them; tell them what you told them."   **INSIGHT**

—oft-repeated advice about how to give a good speech

Beginning.   For many speeches, you will want to follow the same three steps of attention, motivation, and overview that you would use for a teaching lecture.

1. *Attention.*   There are times, however, when such an introduction might not be appropriate. For example, at times an attention step may not be needed. The CEO of an organization talking to his immediate subordinates, a personnel manager of a company talking to employees about the new pay scale for the company, a movie star addressing his fan club, and a prominent family counselor speaking to a group of married couples who chose to attend the talk all have their audiences' attention at the beginning. Still, audience attention is not something that can be taken for granted.

One of America's better known speakers confides that he spends more time on what he refers to as his opening "hook" than on any other part of the talk. He explains that if he can hook the audience's attention at the beginning, he then only needs to keep their attention. Although keeping attention is not always an easy task, it is not as difficult as initially gaining the attention. This speaker will sometimes devote 3 to 5 minutes of a 20-minute talk to his "hook," or attention step. At times, he uses humor or an engaging human interest story or example, but in all cases he sets the stage for the rest of his talk by using attention-getting material that relates directly to the body of the talk. If you can't decide whether you need an attention step in your speech, then you probably do. Most talks will be improved with the addition of an effective attention step.

INSIGHT   *"Open . . . to begat an awful [awesome] attention in the audience."*

—Richard Brinsley Sheridan, Anglo-Irish dramatist

---

2. *Motivation.* Although some sort of attention device is usually needed in a speech, at times a motivation step may be unnecessary. For instance, if your listeners are highly motivated to listen, then a motivation step establishing their need to listen would be out of place or redundant at best. For example, a short time ago, a world-class runner was conducting a local clinic on running. Each participant had paid a substantial fee to attend. This well-known runner did not need to tell the audience why it was important for them to listen. The commitment to listen was already present. Listeners would not have paid their money to listen if they had not believed this expert had some valuable information for them. Much like a briefing, the speaker was able after a very brief introduction to launch quickly into the body of the speech and present hints and techniques helpful to runners. Every good speaker, of course, attempts to motivate listeners throughout the speech. No matter how much credibility you have on the subject or how willing your audience is to listen to you, you have a responsibility to provide continuing motivation for them to listen throughout the talk.

3. *Overview.* The overview step needed in most teaching lectures is unnecessary in many speeches. In fact, with speeches meant to persuade, it often helps to not preview what is to follow, especially if the audience does not initially share your point of view. If speakers tell audiences what they want to persuade them to believe or do, audiences may turn against them before they even begin. Also, the material in some speeches meant to entertain doesn't lend itself to an overview. Generally, in an informative speech, some type of overview is essential, even if the overview consists only of mentioning the main points or of "telling them what you are going to tell them." The best advice is to consider the audience, occasion, and objectives of your speech and then to decide if an overview is appropriate.

Ending. In some speeches, you may choose to use the same three steps of summary, remotivation, and closure appropriate for teaching lectures. As with the introduction, however, the speaking situation will help determine what kind of conclusion is best. Most speeches will not require an extensive conclusion. With informative speeches, you may want to summarize briefly the main points you covered. With persuasive speeches, your conclusion may be a motivating statement of what you want your listeners to believe or how you want them to act. With an entertaining speech, there may be little suitable for summary or motivation.

All kinds of speeches, however, need some type of closure to provide completeness. Most speakers seem to give little thought about how to conclude. You can be assured that the time you spend attending to this detail will be time well spent since it is often the last impression that the audience carries with them.

"It was a good speech. He finished fast."

—overheard

INSIGHT

Exercise	**Beginning and Ending Presentations**

Select a subject you know something about—one that you might speak to an audience about. Assume that in one case you will be giving a briefing, in another case a lecture, and in another a speech. Prepare an appropriate beginning and ending for each type of presentation.

TECHNIQUES FOR GAINING ATTENTION

Techniques for gaining attention at the beginning of a presentation may also be used in the body of the talk, but since the first place a speaker seeks to gain attention is at the beginning, I choose to discuss them here. Different types of talks require different kinds of beginnings. Consider each of these techniques, and use them appropriately, remembering that at times—for example, with briefings—an attention step may be inappropriate or unnecessary.

Question

You may use either open or closed questions to gain audience attention. Both types call for a response. Open ones ask for a response that can be heard or seen; closed ones do not. If you begin with a closed question, such as "What has been the most significant event in your life?" or "How many of you will be injured in automobile accidents within the next five years?" you won't expect audible answers, for the questions are closed or "rhetorical" questions—ones meant to evoke curiosity, provoke thought, or focus attention without eliciting a voiced or demonstrated response. With either question, you expect your audience to think of answers but not to say them out loud.

On the other hand, open questions call for audible or demonstrated answers. A speaker asks, "How many of you have served in the armed services of our country?" Here the show of hands is a demonstrated response—one that can be seen. A coach motivating his players asks, "How many of you think we can beat State on Saturday?" If the noise of the players isn't deafening, the chances aren't good. Sometimes, speakers use open questions to get a unified audience reaction. For example: "Do you want to keep on paying high taxes?" The politician using this question may want the partisan audience to respond in unison, "No!"

Poor questions, both open and closed, are easy to design; good questions are more difficult. "Have you ever wondered how many people drive Chevrolets?" is not a good question. Many people in your audience will reply mentally, "No, and I don't care." "Would you like to earn a million dollars a week?" may also be ineffective since it is pretty far from reality. You should also avoid confusing questions: "How much fuel was used by the U.S. Air Force, the air forces of other Western nations, and all commercial airlines from these countries during the past five years?" Also avoid open questions that may embarrass: "How many of you are deeply in debt?"

Good questions—both open and closed—are clear and direct, and they invite involvement from the audience: "What job do you want in five years?" "If you had one wish, what would it be?" Be prepared! You may ask an open question and the audience doesn't respond openly. You may ask a closed one and they do. The way you ask the question will influence the response. If you preface the question with "Let me see a show of hands. How many _____?" you will most likely get the demonstrated response you want. At times, to prevent voiced or demonstrated response, you might say, "Ask yourself this question: how many _____?" Also, phrasing, pausing, and emphasis can bring the desired audience response. (Chapter 9 treats elements of delivery.)

INSIGHT | *Many speeches are dull because the speaker is asking the wrong questions.*

Quotation

Usually without looking too hard, you can find a quotation by someone both authoritative and popular who is enthusiastic and supports your point of view. Most libraries have copies of the latest edition of Bartlett's *Familiar Quotations.*

Better yet, simply find it and many other sources of quotations on the Internet. That's how I found many of the ones used in this book. There are quotation books and on-line resources especially for teachers, salespeople, speakers, ministers, and others. Also, if you keep your eyes open, you will come across quotations in your day-to-day reading that you can use later on. Make it a practice to copy and file them away for future use. I file quotations on my computer, along with illustrations and other materials I may use in future speeches.

When you use a quotation to open a talk, remember to keep it brief and understandable. You want to gain the audience's attention, not lose it. Make certain the quotation will lead listeners to the content of your talk. Suppose a public-speaking consultant is giving a presentation on how to keep audience attention throughout a speech. He might began this way: "The great American playwright Arthur Miller once said, 'All the plays I tried to write were plays that would grab an audience by the throat and not release them.' Arthur Miller's task is the task you face every time you speak. Today I will tell you how to maintain your audience's full attention—how to grab your audience by the throat and not release them till the end of your speech." By the way, a good title for this speech might be "Grabbing Your Audience by the Throat and Not Letting Go." It's long, but effective.

A speech to a Rotary Club on the importance of a new program to teach reading in the community's public schools might begin this way:

> Thank you for inviting me to speak today on the new reading initiative we are putting in place in our public schools. I am sure each of you Rotarians agrees that reading is crucial to success in life. Certainly, Dr. Rod Paige, the U.S. secretary of education, believes reading is important. Recently, he said, "A child who can read is a child who can learn and succeed, in school and in life." So, Rotarians, today I want to tell you first, how we chose our new program; second, how it is helping our children to learn; and third, how it will help our children succeed in the future.

Notice that the speaker had been invited to speak, so she didn't need a long introduction. She used a very credible—both expert and trustworthy—source for the quotation. She had her audience's attention, provided further motivation by referring to the importance of her subject, and gave a quick but clear overview (notice the speech is organized chronologically); now she is ready to get to the body of her talk. The quotation helped secure attention, and it led into the talk. A quotation used well is an excellent way to gain attention.

Quotations link you, the speaker, to the person being quoted.   **INSIGHT**

Joke

Many speakers would be well advised not to open with a joke. When you buy a joke book from the local bookstore, check one out from the library, or search the Internet, you often find nothing but old gags about in-laws, drunks, and talking horses. A comedian or skilled raconteur can make the jokes funny with appropriate lead-in lines, timing, and putting the story into a believable context. If you do wish to use a joke or humorous story, read the suggestions for using humor given in Chapter 5. Tell the story several times before the talk to people like those who will be in your audience. This practice ensures that you know the joke well and know the kind of response to expect. Also, remember to make sure the story *adds rather than detracts from your talk* by making certain it is *relevant, humorous, and not offensive to your audience.* Many speakers put themselves at serious disadvantage at the beginning of their talks by failing to do these things.

Perhaps the biggest failing of speakers who routinely open with jokes is to neglect to relate them to the speech or situation. There may be times when the most important reason to use humor at the beginning of a talk is to gain audience attention—to get the audience "with you." A joke or the use of other humor—definitions, comparisons, statistics, and such—can be an excellent way to capture attention and create goodwill, but if the humor does not relate to the topic, you have wasted time. On the other hand, humor used effectively at the beginning of a talk does two things—it gains attention, and it leads into the subject of the talk. Most jokes can be made to lead into the talk with good transitions. Notice in the next scenario how a speaker at a Lions Club spouse night (a night when men and women in the club bring their spouses or friend for dinner, fellowship, and fun) uses a humorous story at the beginning of his speech. Notice also that the story is appropriate to this all-adult audience, although it could be questionable if children were in the audience.

Thank you, Bill, for that fine introduction. I'm not sure I deserved all those nice things you said, but I did enjoy hearing them. Perhaps if you knew me better, the introduction would not have been so generous. [pause to let statement soak in—audience most likely smiles at this statement] Perhaps you wouldn't even have invited me. [pause for slight laughter] Sometimes we would do things differently if we knew all the facts. I understand that one evening one of the officers of this club drove his secretary home after work when her car wouldn't start. Although this was an innocent gesture—nothing happened—he decided not to mention it to his wife, who tended to get jealous easily. Later that night, the man and his wife were driving to a restaurant. Suddenly, he looked down and spotted a high-heel shoe half hidden under the passenger seat. Not wanting to be conspicuous, he waited until his wife was looking out her window before he scooped up the shoe and tossed it out of the car. With a sigh of relief, he pulled into the restaurant parking lot. That's when he noticed his wife squirming around in her seat. "Honey," she asked, "have you seen my other shoe?" Sometimes, we don't know all the facts. And maybe if you had known everything about me, I wouldn't be your speaker tonight. But sometimes it's better if we don't know everything. I bet the man didn't tell his wife what happened to the shoe either.

This example shows that at times humor for its own sake may be appropriate even if it is simply to gain the attention and goodwill of the audience. But even then, good transitions will weave the humor into the context of the speech.

Our five senses are incomplete without the sixth—a sense of humor.	**INSIGHT**

Startling Statement

"Tonight, more people will watch the most popular sitcom on TV than have seen all of the stage performances of all of Shakespeare's plays in the last 100 years." This statement happens to be true. "When I was 14 years old I fell in love with a woman 37 feet tall." This statement would be a novel way to start a talk about a 37-foot statue in one's hometown. Remember to make your statement not only startling but also relevant.

A woman speaking on abuse begins her speech by saying, "Most of you know me. You know that my husband and I have three beautiful children, live in a nice home, have good jobs, and are active in this community. Some of you have told me that I seem so fortunate and well adjusted. I agree. I do consider myself very fortunate and pretty well adjusted too. But it hasn't always been that way. For you see, I was abused as a child, and in my first marriage I was a target of spouse abuse. I know that very few of you knew that about me. But I tell you that today, because I want you to know how passionately I feel about abuse of any kind." This statement came as a surprise to her audience, but it reinforced their attention, established her credibility on the subject, and ensured their continued attention as she spoke.

But beware! Startling statements can backfire if they have too much shock value. I once heard a speaker begin, "On my way here tonight, I stopped at the sight of a tragic automobile accident. Two young people were killed—decapitated when they drove under the trailer of an eighteen-wheeler." At this point, people in the audience wondered who it was. Perhaps it was their children or those of their friends. Not only did much of the audience not pay attention to what the speaker said after that, many left the room to call and check on their own children. Others drove to the scene of the accident.

Don't make untrue statements simply to catch audience attention. Once a speaker in a class I was teaching began this way: "I am a prostitute—a woman of the street, the kind of person who attracts some people and nauseates others. Life looks different through my eyes than through yours. Well, that's not really true; I'm not that kind of girl. I'm not a prostitute, but now that I have your attention . . . " She had everyone's attention, but most of the listeners spent the rest of the speech wondering if she was lying when she said she was a prostitute or when she said she wasn't. People acted differently toward her for the rest of the course.

Gimmick

Novelty openings are distinctive, creative, and usually visual. An expert in the use of visual aids once opened his talk on creative visual aids by quickly drawing an attractive picture on the chalkboard and saying, "When we have completed this two-hour block of instruction, I guarantee that you will be able to draw this well." Then he went on to explain that he had predrawn the picture on the board with a pencil and traced it with chalk (a technique I mentioned in the last chapter) and that he was going to show the audience how to use techniques like this to improve their use of visual aids.

Gimmicks such as tearing a $5 bill in half, blowing a loud whistle, or taking off one's coat and hurling it across the room may be illegal, dangerous, or simply not relevant. Think through any gimmick that you plan to use. Try it on a few friends first to get their reaction. Then make certain it is legal, safe, and relevant to your talk.

The most dramatic gimmick I ever witnessed happened in one of my classes in public speaking at the University of Missouri–Columbia in the early 1970s. A student actually used the gimmick at the end of his speech rather than at the beginning. The student concluded his seven-minute speech on depression this way: "So today I hope you have gained a better understanding and appreciation of depression and some of the telltale signs. But you can't always tell who is the most depressed. It may be your roommate, or spouse, or the person sitting next to you in class right now. It may even be me." With that, he hurled himself out of the open window of the third-floor classroom. I nearly had a heart attack as I raced toward the window—fearing for his life and certain I would lose my job for allowing this to happen. I looked down, and there he was lying on an air mattress about four feet below the windowsill on scaffolding he and his buddies had constructed during the night. I was relieved but not amused. I made him repeat the assignment on a different subject with assurances there would be no foolish gimmicks.

> *Gimmicks are often effective until they backfire.*   **INSIGHT**

Common Ground

A speaker establishes common ground by mentioning a common interest relevant to the subject at hand. When conducting training on speaking, writing, and listening to a new Georgia Agri-Leaders Class (farmers and agricultural personnel participating in a yearlong program), as I have done for over a decade, I make certain they know from the start that I was born and raised on a farm in Iowa and that for six years before attending Iowa State University (the state agricultural school), I was a farmer. I do this to make certain they know that I am knowledgeable and sympathetic to their concerns. Even though this part of my background does not apply directly to my ability to teach communication skills, it builds rapport and acceptance. I also use agricultural examples throughout the presentation as a reminder.

When visiting the University of Iowa, where I was once a student, I began: "It is a real pleasure to be in Iowa City, to visit again this university where I received two degrees, and to have the opportunity to renew so many happy and rewarding friendships. It was here that I formed many of my ideas about communication theory and public speaking—ideas that continue to influence me today. I owe much of my success to my experiences both in and outside of the classroom here at the University of Iowa."

Reference

Many times you can gain the audience's attention simply by referring to the occasion, significance of the subject, special interest of the audience, or what a previous speaker has said.

Occasion.   In 1997, during a celebration of the 50th anniversary of the existence of the United States Air Force as a separate military service, a speaker began: "We are assembled to celebrate the 50th birthday of the United States Air Force." A speech commemorating the world's first night flight in Montgomery, Alabama, began: "Today, we are gathered on a very historic spot. It was here at the Wright Brothers Flying School that the first successful night flight in the world was completed."

Subject.   The method of referring to the subject is closely related to the discussion earlier in this chapter about the motivation step in a lecture. The method is simple. Develop the attention around the implied theme: my subject is important to you. Tell listeners why they should listen to you. This approach is often most successful when you don't actually tell the listeners why the subject is important. You simply think of the two or three reasons why the subject is significant, then state and amplify them until the audience reacts favorably. A slight variation is to start something like this: "I know you won't underestimate the importance of what I tell you today, for the subject of _____ concerns everybody."

Special interests. A speaker addressing a local Lions Club known for its support of the Blue–Gray football game each year to raise money for the eye bank program might start: "The Blue–Gray football game is enjoyed annually through nationwide TV. But how many of its viewers know that it is more than a game with some of this country's finest professional prospects? All of us in this room know that this game helps people see."

Previous speaker. When several speakers appear on one occasion, an alert speaker can often shape an opening based on what someone else has already said. This is particularly effective since the reference is fresh in the listeners' minds and gives a sense of spontaneity to the talk. If you use this approach, you can either explain how your subject fits with the previous talk or show a plausible relation between the two. For example: "Dr. Henry just told you how important it is to use effective support in your talks. I am going to speak on something even more basic. I want to suggest how important it is to provide a good organizational framework in which to use the kinds of support Dr. Henry talked about."

Whatever means you use to gain attention—question, quotation, joke, startling statement, gimmick, common ground, reference, or some other means—be sure it is appropriate and leads into your speech. The way you transition from your attention step to the next thing you say sets the tone for the rest of the speech and the transitions that follow. Effective speakers help audiences listen by transitioning easily from one part of a talk to other parts.

INSIGHT	*"It was a great opening, but what did it have to do with anything?"*
	—comment from a listener about a speech

Exercise   Beginning a Speech

Using either a different topic or the same one used in the earlier exercise on beginning and ending presentations, try to use as many different techniques as possible to begin a speech—that is, question, quotation, joke, startling statement, gimmick, and common ground. Would you use different methods for different audiences? Which method works best for your particular speech? Which is easiest? Which is most difficult?

PREPARING EFFECTIVE TRANSITIONS

Transitions are statements used by the speaker to move from the beginning to the body of the talk, between main points, between subpoints, and from the body to the ending of the talk. Transitions signal the audience that you are progressing to a new point, but they are also important in maintaining continuity. Using transitions effectively is one mark of an effective speaker, for transitions add polish to the presentation while they aid listeners. Transitions can be classed by function: mechanical, relational, and summarizing.

Mechanical Transitions

These are the simplest type of transition. At times, nothing else is needed. The speaker who is talking on the "Six Sensational Spots in Seattle" (mentioned in Chapter 2) might say in going from point one to point two, "The second sensational spot is the Woodland Park Zoo." In other words, just a simple signal that she is going from her first point to her second is sufficient. With the speech "The Four E's of Excellent Living" (also in Chapter 2), the speaker might say, "The third E is for Encouragement." While these short mechanical transitions are better than no transitions, usually you will want to use transitions that show a relationship between the two points.

Relational Transitions

As the name implies, relational transitions tie two points or two parts of a speech together by showing a relationship between them. But relational transitions between points do even more. They tie or relate the two points back to the point they are subordinate to—that is, main points are tied back to the objective of the speech, subpoints back to the main point, and sub-subpoints back to the subpoint. For example, the speaker talking on the "Six Sensational Spots in Seattle" might transition from her first to her second point as follows: "I'm sure you understand why I started by telling you about what many consider to be the most sensational spot in Seattle, the Space Needle. Certainly, it is Seattle's most famous landmark. But even more popular with the locals, especially those with children, is the Woodland Park Zoo—one of the most sensational and fun zoos anywhere." With "The Four E's of Excellent Living," the speaker might say, "Enthusiasm—a joy for life—characterizes people who are living excellently. But these excellent livers are also Encouragers."

When going from the overview at the beginning of a speech to the body of the speech, a speaker might say, "So today I want to take a few minutes to share with you what I believe are the six most sensational spots in Seattle. Let's begin with one of the best known, the sensational Space Needle." The transition from the sixth point to the summary might go like this: "Yes, the

Museum of Flight certainly deserves to be included as one of Seattle's six sensational spots. But before I conclude, let me remind you of all six sensational spots we learned about today. We visited . . . " When going from the beginning to the body of the talk on excellence, the speaker might say, "Today I want to look with you at four E's that characterize the lives of people who live excellently. The first E stands for Enlightenment. Certainly, those who pursue excellence seek continuing Enlightenment; they are lifelong learners." The speaker might transition from the last point to the conclusion in this way: "People who live excellently are not only people who are Enlightened, Enthusiastic, and Encouraging, they are people who Endure; they never give up; they hang in there even when times are tough. These then are the marks of Excellence."

In the two previous examples dealing with Seattle and with excellence, the relationships were only sequential—points followed one another. When there's a direct or dependent relationship between points, relational transitions become very important. Consider the following transition from a speech on having a mandatory physical fitness program in the military: "We have discussed the precedents for a mandatory physical fitness program in the military, but these precedents alone will not prove a need for such a program. To more fully understand that need, we must next examine in several practical situations the benefits of mandatory physical fitness." Notice that the relationship transition relates the point just discussed (precedents) to the objective (need for a mandatory program) and introduces the next point (benefits). For relational transitions between points to be effective, they should mention the point just discussed and introduce the next point.

Relational transitions between (1) the beginning and the first point of the body and between (2) the last point and the ending must show those relationships clearly. When planned and used correctly, transitions—especially those between points—act as "mini-summaries" and contribute substantially to the continuity of the total talk. Sometimes, longer summarizing transitions or interim summaries (as contrasted with the final summary used at the end of some talks) help the talk flow clearly.

Summarizing Transitions

Summaries after main points or key ideas are useful tools for maintaining continuity within a talk and for highlighting areas of particular importance. Summarizing transitions or interim summaries are usually not needed. In fact, if the point is very clear, a summary may be unnecessarily redundant and boring. You should use a summary, however, when main points are unusually long or contain complex or unfamiliar information or if it is important to remind listeners of the points you have covered before presenting new information. A summarizing transition or internal summary is actually an expanded relational transition, one that gives more detail about points already covered. Here is a summarizing transition on the previous example of a mandatory physical fitness program:

> We have discussed the precedents for a mandatory physical fitness program in the military. We have seen how the Army, Navy, Air Force, and Marines have all had required physical fitness programs. We have also examined the reasons for such programs and have heard why past commanders of the various branches of the armed services have favored such programs. But precedents alone will not prove a need for such a program. To more fully understand that need, we must next examine in several practical situations the benefits of mandatory physical fitness.

Notice how this summarizing transition gives more detail than the shorter relational transition. The speaker here reminds listeners of more detail.

Exercise   Using Transitions

If you did either of the exercises in Chapter 6 on making and using flipcharts or PowerPoint slides, add appropriate transitions to the mini-talks you prepared. If not, simply take the points given for each exercise and tie them together with appropriate transitions. First, use mechanical transitions; next, use relational transitions; and finally, try to construct appropriate summarizing transitions. While these simple points may not really require relational or summarizing transitions, the discipline of constructing them will help you in the future.

Exercise   The Group Speech

Start with a topic that can easily be organized into main points—for example, the three branches of federal government, the advantages and disadvantages of something, or the three most important events of the past century. Assign various parts of the speech to different participants. For example, with nine participants, the parts might be Attention, Motivation, Overview, Main Point 1, Main Point 2, Main Point 3, Summary, Remotivation, and Closure. With a larger number of participants, some may be assigned to provide supporting material for points made. Allow no time for planning, but have each participant get up and talk at the appropriate time. Tape-record the speech. After the speech is completed, play it back and discuss the product. Then allow participants several minutes to brainstorm each part and plan *transitional* sentences and phrases to present a single unified speech.

AFTER PREPARATION, THEN WHAT?

The first seven chapters of this book have discussed how to prepare; how to organize; how to use clarification, proof, and humorous and visual support; and how to begin, end, and tie parts of a talk together with effective transitions. What comes next is the most frightening part for many people—the actual presentation of the talk. Actually, it's the fun part. Chapter 8 tells how to deliver the talk.

Check Yourself: What Have You Learned?

- ☐ Beginnings and endings should fit the audience, the speaker, and the type of talk you are giving.
- ☐ Since briefings are to be brief, lengthy beginnings and endings are inappropriate.
- ☐ Beginnings of lectures should generally have attention, motivation, and overview steps.
- ☐ Endings of lectures should generally have summary, remotivation, and closure steps.
- ☐ Speeches may also use the same beginning and ending steps as lectures.
- ☐ Techniques to gain attention at the start of a talk include:
  - Questions, both open (which invite a voiced or other demonstrated response) and closed (which do not invite a voiced response)
  - Quotations
  - Jokes
  - Startling statements
  - Gimmicks
  - Establishment of common ground
  - Reference to occasion, subject, special interests, or a previous speaker
- ☐ Transitions between beginning and body, between body and ending, or between other parts of the speech may be:
  - Mechanical
  - Relational
  - Summarizing

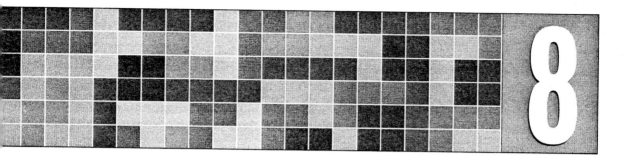

Presentation Strategies

OBJECTIVE

■ To apply presentational strategies to your own talks

TASKS

■ Tell strengths and weaknesses of the four methods of presentation.

■ Discuss the guidelines for preparing a manuscript and speaking from it.

■ Explain why the extemporaneous method works best in most situations.

■ Demonstrate the differences between a preparation outline and a presentation outline.

■ Explain how to effectively answer questions from the audience.

■ Tell how a speaker can control nervousness.

Although preparing a talk can be laborious, putting it all together for presentation presents a challenge for most speakers. You may have outstanding content with a good organization pattern, strong supporting material, and a well-planned beginning and ending. You may have even planned excellent transitions to tie the parts together. But now you look at what you have and wonder what is the best strategy for presentation? What kind of notes should you use? What if the audience asks questions? Should you plan a question-and-answer period? How can you overcome nervousness? This chapter answers these questions and more.

PRESENTATION APPROACHES

Speakers can use one of four common presentation approaches: (1) speaking from memory, (2) reading from a manuscript, (3) speaking impromptu with no specific preparation, and (4) speaking extemporaneously with, ideally, a great deal of preparation and a limited number of notes. The fourth method will allow you the most freedom in adjusting to an audience and is best suited for most speaking.

Memorizing

Speaking from memory is the poorest method of delivering talks, and it should be used very sparingly, if at all. While this method may seem to help persons who can't think on their feet, the memorized talk is a straitjacket. It won't allow you to adjust to the audience and the situation. Moreover, the method is almost sure to destroy spontaneity and a sense of communication, except perhaps with experienced actors. The method also requires an inordinate amount of preparation, and the danger of forgetting the content is ever present.

INSIGHT | *There are three important things to remember about speaking from memory: it destroys spontaneity, requires an inordinate amount of preparation, and uh, uh, I can't remember the other thing.*

Manuscript Reading

Reading a talk from a manuscript—that is, writing out the entire speech and reading it—allows you to plan the exact words and phrases to use. In some formal speeches, especially those to be made available to the media (such as those by important dignitaries or heads of state), a fully written-out speech is a necessity. Certainly when the U.S. president addresses millions of people by television and there is no room for a misstatement, a manuscript is crucial.

But in most cases, the disadvantages of this method of presentation far outweigh the advantages. Many speakers use the manuscript as a crutch instead of fully thinking through the ideas in the talk. All too often, the written talk is regarded simply as an essay to be read aloud. Therefore, the talk is too broad and has language that is too abstract to be understood when presented orally. Some people claim that they want the manuscript there for security but that they will use it as they would use notes rather than read from it. Most people would be much better off if they used the extemporaneous method described later—that is, a carefully prepared speech given from a brief outline or notes. But even with extemporaneous speaking, at times you may have to read quotations or some other documentation. If you must read, consider the following suggestions.

Prepare the Manuscript

Follow these guidelines when preparing the manuscript for your talk:

- Understand that spoken words should be simpler, clearer, and more vivid than in writing.
- Make sure sentences are shorter and ideas less complex than in writing.
- Understand that transitions between thoughts and ideas need to be clear. Provide signposts to keep the audience from getting lost. Reread the discussion in Chapter 7 about how to use transitions effectively.
- Use repetition to emphasize main ideas and key points.
- Use direct address when speaking about people. Personal pronouns, such as *I, we, our, us,* and *you,* are better than *they, people, a person, the reader,* and *the hearer.*
- Use concrete language where possible. Follow abstract or complicated reasoning with specific examples, comparisons, and definitions. This is important in all speaking but is imperative when speaking from a manuscript.

Prepare a Reading Draft

Your "reading draft" should be readable as you stand to present. Here are some guidelines:

- Use as large a type as practical to increase visibility and readability.
- Use serif fonts or typeface. In Chapter 6, I said that serif fonts might not work as well as sans serif fonts for visuals. But serifs help when reading from a printed page. The serifs—little lines at the top and bottom of the letters—help guide the eye from letter to letter.
- Use boldface or underlining to highlight important words you want to emphasize.
- Double or triple space to make the words stand out more clearly and reduce the chance of confusion or misreading of the text.
- Write out words phonetically if they are difficult to pronounce or may in some way cause you to stumble. Or, put the correct pronunciation in parentheses immediately following a difficult word.

- Type on only one side of the paper for easier handling.
- Mark your manuscript, perhaps using vertical lines between words where you wish to pause. Underscore words you want to emphasize. Some speakers use double and triple vertical lines or underlining for added emphasis.
- Mark places in the manuscript where you plan to use visual aids.
- Use short paragraphs to reduce the chance of losing your place.
- Number your pages with large numerals in the upper righthand corner so you can quickly put them in order if you drop them. I once heard a speaker go from page one to page three without knowing he had skipped page two. Only after he was finished and it was brought to his attention did he realize what had happened.

INSIGHT

A minister was reading from Genesis 3:7—"They sewed fig leaves together and made themselves skirts." Then, as the minister leafed over to the next page, he accidentally skipped a page and continued reading from Genesis 6:2: "The men took notice of the women and admired their looks." Just then the minister exclaimed, "I think we lost a leaf here."

Practice the Talk

Read your talk aloud to see how it sounds. Here are some guidelines for practicing your talk:

- Record yourself on a cassette recorder and listen to the playback to help you discover places where you may not be communicating effectively.
- Consider videotaping your presentation to see how you look reading it.
- Read and reread the talk several times, perhaps once a day for several days, if you have time.
- Try to make your talk sound like conversation, as if you were thinking the words for the first time as you read them.
- Avoid combinations of words that are difficult to say. Make necessary changes on the manuscript.
- Practice looking at your audience most of the time as the manuscript becomes more familiar to you.
- Provide punctuation with vocal inflection, variety, and pauses.
- Think about what you are saying as if it were the first time you said the words.

Presenting the Talk

Use one of two methods for handling the manuscript. (1) Hold the manuscript in front of you with one hand high enough so that you can see it without bending your head, but not high enough to hide your face. The other hand will be free to change pages and gesture. (2) Place the manuscript on a speaker's stand or table so that both hands are free to gesture. Make sure, however, that the manuscript is placed high enough to read from without bending over. This is very important. Sometimes books or other objects may be used to raise the manuscript to the desired height. Whichever approach is used, remember to *let the eyes, not the head, drop to the paper.*

- Don't explain why you choose to read the talk. If you have prepared well, you should do a good job and no apologies will be necessary.

- Be willing to change the wording here and there as you go along if it will help you communicate ideas to your hearers. These changes will make delivery more conversational.

- Insert comments of up to a sentence or two in length to add variety, but be careful not to deviate so far from the manuscript that your train of thought is interrupted. You should have carefully thought through and prepared the manuscript. Last-minute changes and impromptu asides can be confusing for both you and your hearers.

- Be flexible enough that you can shorten the talk, if necessary. It's frustrating to have a 30-minute talk and then learn that you have only 20 minutes to present it. Rushing through it is not the answer; know in advance where you can cut it.

- Let pauses be dictated by ideas. Pause wherever there would normally be a pause in the same language in informal conversation. You will need to pause often, even when the written punctuation does not dictate a pause.

- Concentrate on the meaning and ideas rather than on individual words. If you have written your own talk, you are intimate with the ideas and the words you have chosen to express those ideas. You built the talk; you should understand it. Therefore, the most helpful aid to good delivery is to re-create the feeling that helped you put the words on paper. Speak no passage until its meaning hits your mind.

- Construct the next idea in your mind before uttering it.

- Read with the sincerity, enthusiasm, directness, and force that are proper to the occasion.

- Use gestures, and look directly at the audience when executing them.

A manuscript talk, then, is not, as someone once said, merely "an essay on its hind legs." The manuscript should be written in a conversational tone rather than in formal English. A talk is meant to be heard, not read. If you prepare well, practice diligently, and attend to the factors of delivery, you can usually read very acceptably and spontaneously.

> **INSIGHT** *Reading from a script may reduce pressure for the speaker, but it often sounds like a book rather than a talk.*

Impromptu Speaking

Impromptu speaking requires a tremendous amount of skill and knowledge. You may find it necessary at times to talk on the spur of the moment without any preparation. But only experienced speakers who are saturated with their subjects and who have the ability to organize their thoughts for learning as they speak should use this method. Even these experienced speakers fall back on thoughts and phrases they have used before. They have spent years, so to speak, in preparing to give an unprepared talk.

> **INSIGHT** *"I spent a long time preparing those 'off the cuff' remarks."*
>
> —noted speaker

Extemporaneous Speaking

Effective speakers use the technique of extemporaneous speaking the most. Extemporaneous speaking produces the most fruitful results when it is based on full preparation and adequate practice. The talk is carefully planned and outlined in detail. Your only guide is usually a well-constructed outline. It is a talk planned idea by idea rather than word by word.

There are many advantages to speaking from a well-planned outline. Outlining compels you to organize ideas and causes you to weigh materials in advance. It gives you freedom to adapt a talk to the occasion and to adjust to audience reactions. It enables you to change what you plan to say right up to the moment of utterance. In short, the extemporaneous method will help you accomplish the two vital needs of effective speaking: adequate preparation and a lively sense of communication.

In Chapter 2, you saw examples of two planning outlines—one on "Native Tribes in the West" and another on "Nonverbal Communication." The planning outline will help you as you gather your material. After you have your material, you will most likely want to construct a *preparation outline*—one that includes all the points, the supporting material, the beginning, the ending, and perhaps even connectors or transitions that tie the material together. In short, the preparation outline contains everything needed to enable you to come back to your talk and give it again later. After you have finished your preparation outline, you'll want to prepare a *presentation outline* (sometimes called a keyword outline). This is the outline you'll use when you actually present the talk. In most cases, it will be considerably shorter than the preparation outline and will contain key words or phrases to remind you of main points, subpoints, and supporting material you plan to use, as well as the things you want to include in the beginning and ending of the talk. It should fit on one page or be written on no more than three or four index cards so you can use it when you actually give your talk.

Figure 8.1 is a preparation outline. I prepared it following the planning outline shown in Chapter 2 for the talk on "Nonverbal Communication." *You may choose to construct a more complete preparation outline in which you write out more of your supporting material.* (For example, in point IA1b, I didn't write out the humorous example of the man attempting to buy something from a street vendor in Athens. I witnessed it and will be able to remember it with this short prompt.) I constructed this outline confident I could return to it a year later and present the talk again. Notice that I stayed with the same main points and subpoints as in the planning outline. But as I gathered material, I changed the sub-subpoints under the first main point of Internal Factors. Why did I change them?

A planning outline is just that—a plan, not a straitjacket. Material you gather may suggest changes in organization and presentation. Notice also that I gave the talk a new title. I use a question: "What Are You Doing?" Notice how I plan to use the title to capture attention at the beginning and to provide closure at the end of the talk. *I wouldn't generally write designators such as "clustered example," "testimony," and "definition" on the outline itself*—I labeled my supporting material in Figure 8.1 (1) to show how I used various kinds of support and (2) to emphasize the importance of supporting material. Supporting material is crucial to good speaking. That's why four chapters in this book treat the use of supporting material. Good support is the heart of good presentations.

Figure 8.2 gives the presentation outline for the talk. I generally use no more than one card for an entire presentation. You may find that until you gain more experience, your notes may need to be more detailed than mine. If I have quotations or complex statistics, I place them on *other* cards. Picking up a card and reading a quotation to my audience adds credibility. This practice shows I thought the material was important enough to have it typed and placed on a card by itself—and that I am reading it instead of quoting from memory, where there is a chance to get it wrong.

Subject: Nonverbal Communication
Title: What Are You Doing?
Purpose: To inform
Objective: TOOTSIFELT know the importance of
                  nonverbal factors of communication.

ATTENTION:

"What are you doing?" Has somebody ever asked you that
question? Have you asked somebody else? People watch what
we do. In fact, you've heard it said that "actions speak louder
than words," and most of us would agree.

- Nonverbal behavior—our actions and response to nonverbal
  cues communicate powerfully.
- **[Short example or instance]** This certainly was the case
  with me last week. (Dinner jacket story)

MOTIVATION:

Since we affect others more by our nonverbal behavior than by
what we say verbally, we need to take a closer look at how we
communicate nonverbally. Just how much do we communicate
nonverbally?

- **[Testimony & statistic]** "65 percent of our influence is
  nonverbal."—Dr. Ray Birdwhistle, *Kinesics and Context,*
  University of PA
- Affects all our relationships—home, work, social, school

OVERVIEW:

We can divide nonverbal behavior into two categories—internal
and external.

- **[Definition]** Internal includes all the ways we communicate
  with our body—face, hands, posture, and such. External
  includes everything else.
- Today, we'll first look at internal nonverbal communication—
  specifically our upper, middle, and lower body. Second, we'll
  consider three important aspects of external nonverbal
  communication—objects, space, and time.

FIGURE 8.1 Preparation outline.

BODY OF THE PRESENTATION:

I. Know the internal factors of nonverbal communication.

A. **[Clustered example]** Upper Body (Capitalized on by television newscasters; important when sitting behind a desk, such as at an interview. Most eye contact is directed toward the other person's face.)

   1. Head movement

      a. **[Comparison & contrast]** Cultural differences (nodding the head up and down in most Western cultures means "yes." In Greece and in Bulgaria, means "no.")

      b. **[Humorous example]** Story of man attempting to buy something from a street vendor in Athens

      c. Most powerful internal nonverbal meaning comes from head, including eyes and face

   2. Eye contact

      a. **[Long example or illustration]** Shows interest in others (story about blind friend)

      b. **[Short example/instance]** Provides feedback (importance of audience feedback to speaker)

      c. **[Testimony]** Enhances credibility (results of University of Missouri studies)

   3. Facial expression

      a. **[Visual demonstration/support]** Expresses emotion (show pictures demonstrating fear, happiness, sadness, surprise, etc., and ask listeners to identify emotions expressed)

      b. **[Comparison & contrast]** Although cultures differ, a smile is universally understood. Though in different cultures, there may be different reasons for smiling. Japanese smile when confused or angry; in many parts of Asia and other places, people smile when embarrassed. In some countries and cultures, a smile is reserved for friends. And some smiling that we do may be considered inappropriate in other cultures.

B. Middle Body

1. **[Visual support & example or illustration]** Arms (demonstrate, then tell "big fish story")

2. Hands

a. **[Visual support]** Along with arms, the major means of gesturing (demonstrate)

b. **[Visual demonstration/support & comparison/ contrast]** Cultural differences (beckoning with index finger—demonstrate—means "come here" to us, but it's considered demeaning and even obscene in some cultures. Expect an unexpected reaction from many Asians, Portuguese, Spanish, and even some Latin Americans. And the "V for victory" sign with the palm away from you means "victory" throughout most of Europe, but don't turn your palm toward you; you'll be making an obscene gesture to many Europeans. Hands communicate differently in different places.)

3. Torso

a. **[Visual demonstration/support]** Shoulders, chest, stomach work with arms and hands (demonstrate so listeners can understand how they work together)

b. **[Example/illustration/humor?]** Tell how "Belly Dancers" train (In spite of what some folks think, they don't learn their skill at a naval academy, but they do practice and they do communicate nonverbally.)

C. Lower Body

a. **[Examples]** Hips (Belly dancers also use them; master was Elvis Presley—tell how first time on the Ed Sullivan Show cameras were not allowed to show him from waist down.)

b. **[Comparison]** Legs (support us and all we do; compare with foundation of building)

c. **[Visual support]** Feet (demonstrate different angles, toe out, pigeon toe, etc.; imitate walks of well-known people such as John Wayne.)

FIGURE 8.1   Continued

II. Know the external factors of nonverbal communication

   A. Objects

      1. Present (now)—things that we have around us daily

         a. **[Clustered examples]** Possessions and personal items—clothes we wear, automobiles we drive, things in our home, objects on our desk or at our workplace (Talk about what I'm wearing now, hold up my car keys and other personal items. Ask listeners to consider what they are wearing. Point out something particularly attractive that someone in the audience is wearing. Comment that the person probably gave some thought to wanting to look nice today and add, "They do.")

         b. **[Clustered examples]** Places we go because we enjoy them and perhaps also because we want to be seen there—opening of a new theatre, at the football game, in church (Our association with edifices and objects in and around them communicates something about us. We like plays, athletic events, worship services. And we want to be seen participating.)

         c. What do your objects communicate about you? (rhetorical question inviting thought)

      2. Past—things we have made or done leave evidence of us

         a. **[Example & comparison]** Visited Europe and the great cathedrals and artwork (Show picture of Westminster Abbey and ask if anybody else has been there. Ask what the Abbey tells about the people who constructed it. Display reproductions of great artwork, again asking audience to think about what they say about the artist. Remind them they also leave evidence of where they have been—and what they leave communicates much about them, nonverbally.)

         b. **[Visual support]** Object I made when I was 14 still communicates years later

B. Space

  1. Personal

    a. **[Comparison & example]** Cultural differences between the United States and other countries (Consider Turkey, Korea, Middle Eastern countries, etc. Explain how influx of Koreans into local area with building of new Hyundai plant will make us more aware of differences. Tell recent instance.)

    b. **[Short instance]** Bubble concept—not to infringe on certain area around us (Again cultural differences. Even differences within cultures. Some people are "huggers," some are not.)

    c. **[Statistics & testimony]** Acceptable distances (cite statistics from Edward Hall's *Silent Language:* Intimate: 0–18", Personal: 18"–4', Social: 4'–10', Public Distance: 10' and more)

  2. Perceived

    a. **[Example or instance]** Not actual difference (May live and sleep just inches from someone on the other side of an apartment wall, yet never see them or feel close to them. May see another person come out of the apartment across the hall often. We see them and talk to them without ever getting as physically close to them as the person who sleeps on the other side of the wall.)

    b. **[Clustered examples]** We construct distance (Build walls, block phone calls, arrange office furniture and partitions, all to control distance between others and us.)

  3. Time

    a. **[Clustered example]** Pervasive in our language (Spend time, waste time, get places on time; we are early, late, punctual; next year, next month, last century, now.)

    b. **[Humorous example]** We judge people on how they respect our time. ("I've been waiting for her for 20 minutes." "You're early, I'm not ready for you yet." Story about husband and wife.)

FIGURE 8.1 Continued

c. [**Humorous support**] In fact, some of you are looking at your watches, which probably means that my time is about up. I don't mind when people in the audience sneak a look at their watches; what bothers me is when they do a double take, then take them off and shake them.

SUMMARY:

So whether it is internal nonverbal communication—head, eyes, and face—or external nonverbal factors—the objects around us, the way we respect space, and our use of time—nonverbal communication is an important force affecting how we live with and relate to others. People are continually judging us by what they see about us even more than by what they hear us say.

REMOTIVATION AND CLOSURE:

This fact causes us to stop and think about what we do, where we are, and what we communicate nonverbally about what's important to us. Ask yourself this question: If somebody says one thing and does another, what do you believe—what she said or what she did? I think I know how you would answer that question. We watch what people do. As someone once said, "What you are speaks so loudly that I can't hear what you say"—what you are *doing* communicates more powerfully than what you are *saying*. Actions really do speak louder than words. ***What are you doing?*** Think about it, and you will do a better job of communicating nonverbally.

FIGURE 8.1 Continued

What are you doing? Actions speak louder—dinner jacket story
Dr. Ray Birdwhistle, *Kinesics and Contexts,* U of PA—65%
Defn: *Internal* includes all the ways we communicate with our
         bodies—face, hands, posture, etc.
         External includes everything else./Overview

INTERNAL
UPPER BODY, examples

- Head movement: cultural—head   nod—Gr and Bulg—
  Athens—powerful communication
- Eye contact: interest—blind friend—feedback—credibility—U of
  Mo studies
- Facial expression: emotions—universal smile

MIDDLE BODY

- Arms: fish story
- Hands: demonstrate—cultural differences, beckoning, victory
- Torso: demonstrate, belly dancers/naval academy

LOWER BODY
-Hips: belly dancers and Elvis on Ed Sullivan Show
-Legs: like foundation of building
-Feet: demonstrate

EXTERNAL
OBJECTS
-Present: possessions—personal items—places we go to see
and be seen—Ask audience
-Past: Europe cathedrals and artwork; Abbey—paintings—
object I made at 14

SPACE
-Personal: cultural diff—Hyundai—bubble—"huggers"—Ed
Hall—Intimate 0–18″/Personal 18″–4′/Social 4′–10′/Public > 10′
-Perceived: apartment example; construct distances

TIME
-Pervades language and judgment of others—watch/shake

SUMMARY—REMOTIVATE—CLOSE
Say one thing, do another. What you are . . . Actions speak.
What are you doing?

FIGURE 8.2   Presentation outline.

Q & A: QUESTIONS FROM THE AUDIENCE, ANSWERS FROM YOU

Some talks may generate questions speakers are expected to answer. Briefings, sales presentations, and lectures often require speakers to field questions from listeners. Sometimes these questions come during the talk itself; in other cases, they may come at the end of the presentation. At the beginning of your talk, you may ask listeners to save their questions until the end, or you may encourage them to ask questions as they arise during the presentation. If you take questions during the presentation, feedback will be immediate and you will maintain audience attention. On the other hand, you may get off schedule and have to rush to finish in the allotted time. If you take questions only at the end of the presentation, you maintain control of time but place yourself in an awkward position if audience members want to ask questions during the presentation.

You don't need to know all the answers; no one is smart enough to ask you all the questions.	**INSIGHT**

The choice of whether or not to answer questions during the presentation may not be yours. The trend with business presentations is to ask questions during the presentation. If you have stated your preference to take questions at the end and listeners interrupt with questions during your presentation, then you have a choice—answer them or delay. Generally, it's better to answer unless you plan to cover that point later in the talk. If you do plan to cover it, tell the questioner and ask if the answer can wait until then. Generally, questioners will wait. But if they respond that they would like an answer now, then give it to them. Remember, all speaking is listener centered. Give listeners what they want, and you'll be more likely to get what you want—a sale, a fair hearing, or some other desired response.

The choice of whether or not to answer questions during the presentation may not be yours.	**INSIGHT**

Here are some things to consider about handling questions from an audience—including both how to deal with the questions and how to give good responses.

How to Deal with Questions

Review the information given in Chapter 1 on how to deal with hostile audiences. Most questioners will not be hostile, but the suggestions are good to keep in mind when answering questions from any audience. Here are some other considerations:

1. *Prepare for their questions.* Many experienced presenters practice their presentations in front of "murder boards"—a group of friends or people from their own organization who purposely ask difficult and demanding questions. This is good practice and preparation for the speaker.

2. *Project a positive, warm, polite, friendly image.* Smile. Treat your questioners the way you would want to be treated if you were in their place. Convey the attitude that you welcome their questions.

3. *Restate the question to show you understand.* This is especially important if the question is complex or if it can't be heard by other people in the audience. You might say something like, "So what you are asking is . . ." or "Let me see if I understand your question . . ."

4. *Ask for clarification if you don't understand the question.* Blame yourself, not the questioner, for your not understanding. Never make the questioner look bad.

5. *Even if the question is silly, treat it as though it were a good one.* In one instance, an audience member asked a stupid question. The speaker told the audience that he thought the question was stupid and said that the man who asked it was ill informed. He probably was. But he was also the brother-in-law of the CEO of the company where the speaker was employed. The fallout was not pretty.

6. *Reshape the question if it is unclear or could provide a trap for you.* Consider the following types of troublesome questions:

- *Vague.* Questioners may use unclear terms such as *it, they,* or *this.* For example, "What would be the effect of it?" You reshape the question to show you understand: "You're asking what the effect will be when we implement the new policy. Here is what will . . ."

- *Broad.* If asked a question far too broad to answer in the given time, quickly narrow it. This tactic also allows you to *focus* on what you consider to be important. You are asked the question "What are the best places in the world to visit?" You may answer, "Certainly you will go to one of the most popular places if you take this cruise I am going to tell you about next. That's why . . ."

- *Forced choice.* In effect, the questioner is attempting to limit your options by making you choose between two things. "Do you favor raising taxes to help our schools or to improve our highways?" You may not favor raising taxes for any reason. Or, you may wish to raise them to help both schools and highways. But the questioner is attempting to make you choose between two alternatives. In response, simply state your position: "I do not favor raising taxes at this time for any reason." Or, "I believe we need more revenue for both."

- *Leading.*   The questioner attempts to lead you to the answer he wants. "Wouldn't you agree that the falling value of Acme stock points to real problems in the company?" You answer, "Not at all. If you will look at the value of Acme stock over the past 20 years, you'll find that it has consistently outperformed the market and continues to do so. It's actually stronger in comparison to the overall market than it has been in the last five years." In other words, instead of getting trapped by a leading question, you use it to your advantage.

- *Loaded.*   The two previous questions—forced choice and leading— were also "loaded" with emotionally charged language. Loaded questions use emotion to put "twist" on the question. Don't let it trap you.

How to Give Good Responses

The previous list on dealing with questions also gives ideas on responses. Here are some more suggestions:

- *Keep the entire audience involved.*   Don't look only at the asker when answering the question. Look at others in the audience. Give them the kind of direct yet impartial eye contact we discuss later in Chapter 9. Also, don't spend a long time answering a specific question that holds no interest for the rest of the audience.

- *Take questions from different parts of the room.*   Try to follow a question from one side of the room with one from the other side. Don't just work one part of the audience.

- *With necessarily longer answers, follow the guidelines on organization presented in Chapter 2.*   For example, you might say, "Yes, I have three concerns about the new procedure. First . . . "

- *Make answers as short as possible yet long enough to answer the question.*

- *Remember your TOOTSIFELT—your objective—as discussed in Chapter 1.* Make your answers support your objective. Think of your answers as adding supporting material to points you made.

- *If you don't know the answer, say so.* Tell questioners where they can find the answer, or ask them to give you a phone number or e-mail address after the talk and promise to get back to them. Then do it soon.

- *Remember that the questions and answers either during the talk or following it are part of the total presentation.* Therefore, points covered throughout this book also apply to the question-and-answer part of a presentation.

INSIGHT	*Q & A is where you really get down to what the audience wants to know.*

CONTROLLING NERVOUSNESS

If you suffer from stage fright, nervousness, or fear of speaking—and you show it—your audience may also become uneasy or anxious. Yet some nervousness is both natural and desirable. While you may not be able to eliminate nervousness, the secret is to control it. Even skilled speakers often experience the queasy feeling of "butterflies in the stomach" as they prepare to speak. The old adage is to get the butterflies "flying in formation." It's not always that easy, but there are things you can do.

INSIGHT	*What do butterflies get in their stomachs when they're nervous?*

Practice, practice, practice. Just as a visiting athletic team practices on a field before game time to accustom themselves to differences in terrain and environment, so you may need to "dry run" or practice your talk several times, preferably in the room where the talk will be given, before actually presenting it. Practice reminds us to look up the pronunciation of a word that is new or check an additional piece of information on an important point. Practice builds confidence.

INSIGHT	*Practice builds confidence.*

Be interested in your subject. At times, you may talk on subjects that you find dull, but as you get more involved, the subject becomes more interesting. There is no such thing as a dull subject, only dull speakers. It is important to be enthusiastic about your subject, because enthusiasm can replace fear.

And the more enthusiastic you are about the subject, the more involved the audience will be, both with you and what you are saying. Audience involvement will reduce your fear and contribute to the success of your talk.

> *"The man who is pleading his own cause before a large audience will be more readily listened to."*
>
> —Titus Livius

INSIGHT

Release nervous energy before you speak.   Walking, jogging, or other physical activity are good tactics. They clear your mind and release negative nervous energy. (*Note:* Nervous energy is not the same as the positive energy or dynamism discussed in Chapter 9.) You'll speak more effectively if you release nervous energy shortly before the presentation. For some people, a nap helps, although most people are too nervous to sleep before they speak. If nervousness is a problem, limit or abstain from caffeine for several hours before the presentation. Never drink alcohol to calm your nerves before a presentation. Even prescribed drugs may present a problem. Know their effects. For example, antihistamines and excessive use of tranquilizers leave some people drowsy or dull-witted.

Know the place.   If you haven't had a chance to practice there, at least become familiar with the place you will speak. Arrive early, and stand where you will be speaking. If you will be using a microphone, practice speaking into it if you have the opportunity. Examine the room and walk around where people will be seated. Visualize yourself speaking; imagine yourself confidently facing the audience; and imagine your voice as clear, crisp, and communicative.

Hold good thoughts toward your audience.   The listeners in the audience are the same ones whom you enjoy speaking with in a less structured environment. Most audiences are made up of warm human beings who are interested in what you have to say. They rarely boo or throw vegetables. Most listeners have great empathy for speakers and want them to do a good job.

> *"Sir, if you're not nervous about the speech you are about to give, why did you just butter your tie?"*

INSIGHT

Don't use too many notes.   While speakers often like the comfort of many notes, aside from manuscript speaking, excessive notes generally hinder the presentation. First, they are distracting to the audience. Second, they often distract speakers who shuffle through them to find what they plan to say. Third, they limit eye contact and involvement with the audience. Remember, mutual involvement between you and your audience reduces your fear and contributes to your speaking success.

Don't rush as you begin to speak.   Many speakers are so anxious to get started that they begin before they are ready. The little extra time taken to look at the audience, smile, thank the person for introducing you (if you were introduced), and arrange your notes will generally pay big dividends. When you are ready to begin, look at various parts of the audience, take a deep breath, and begin to speak confidently. If you have a good beginning, the kind discussed in Chapter 7, don't "blow it" by rushing through it. You can gain the audience's goodwill and support at the beginning of the talk. This will reduce nervousness.

Concentrate on your audience and your message.   Put other things out of your mind. You have worked hard on your presentation. If you have followed the advice in the previous chapters, you have had your audience in mind as you prepared. You organized your talk for them. You selected supporting material to appeal to them. You designed the beginning and ending specifically for this audience. You have a message and an audience that needs to hear it. And you are ready to deliver it. This is what you've been waiting for. Just think about the listeners and what you want to say.

Don't apologize for being nervous.   Most of the time your nervousness is not that apparent to the audience, so don't call attention to it. If you remain silent about it, they may never know. Besides, as you get into your talk, you will become so focused on presenting your exciting message to this group of good listeners that you'll forget about being nervous. This is almost always the case if you prepare well with the audience in mind.

Don't let little things bother you.   A slide that is out of sync, a mispronounced word, a door that opens in the back of the room—every time you triumph over these little adversities, you endear yourself to the audience and you gain confidence in yourself. If you stumble over a word, just stop and say it right. If, after a couple of attempts, you still can't say it right, just say something like "Pronunciation was never my strongest suit," or "I just washed my mouth this morning and can't do a thing with it," or "You get the idea." And do it with a smile—not a nervous laugh. A smile wins them every time.

Exercise   Releasing Nervous Tension

You can perform the first two exercises alone or with someone else watching. The value of someone watching is that the other person can observe to make certain you do all the steps correctly.

Head Drooping

Step 1: Sitting or standing, close your eyes and concentrate on "feeling."

Step 2: Try to feel the balance of your head on your shoulders, and search for the precise point where it seems to be weightless.

Step 3: Now let your head fall smoothly (without a jerk) to a fully forward position. You should feel some pull across your shoulders on both sides.

Step 4: Let your head hang free in this position and count to 10. Next, bring it back to the start position, and then let your head go back as far as possible. Repeat this process several times.

Neck

Step 1: Sit in a straight-backed chair.

Step 2: Place the heels of both hands on your forehead above the eyebrows with the fingers facing upward.

Step 3: Slowly press your head forward against the resistance of your hands. Maintain this steady, moderate pressure, count to three, and release the pressure without removing your hands from your head. Wait five seconds, and repeat the procedure. Repeat the procedure three or four times.

Talk to the Wall, Not to the Audience

Step 1: With a cooperative audience, stand in front of them and then turn your back to them and face the wall.

Step 2: Talk to the wall, ignoring the fact that the audience is sitting behind you and listening to you.

Step 3: When you have finished, go to the back of the room with the audience still facing forward and deliver your talk again, facing their backs.

Step 4: When you have finished, tell the audience some of the things you felt while first talking to the wall and then talking to their backs. Then ask what they felt while you had your back to them and what they felt when you talked to their backs.

Recently I listened to one of the greatest motivational speakers in America, Zig Ziegler. Although there were several distractions during the speech, he was unfazed. At one point, he couldn't get the words to come out quite right. He just laughed at himself and went on. He had the audience in the palm of his hand. Learn from the experts. They don't let little things keep them from delivering the message to a waiting audience.

READY FOR THE PRESENTATION

You've done all the work. You've prepared, organized, and supported your talk. You have a good beginning and an ending and have decided what method of presentation to use. You've given careful thought to how to handle a question-and-answer period and are doing all you can to control your nervousness. Now you are ready to present your talk. But before you do, think about your presentational skills. They are the subject of the final chapter.

Check Yourself: What Have You Learned?

- ☐ Speaking from memory limits your ability to adjust to the audience and presents the possibility of forgetting.

- ☐ While at times necessary, speaking from a manuscript often inhibits spontaneity.

- ☐ Only skilled and knowledgeable speakers should speak impromptu, with no preparation.

- ☐ Most effective speakers speak extemporaneously after careful preparation.

- ☐ Planning outlines, preparation outlines, and presentation outlines each serve useful functions for speakers.

- ☐ Speakers need to acquire skill in handling questions from the audience.

- ☐ Nervousness is natural and can be channeled.

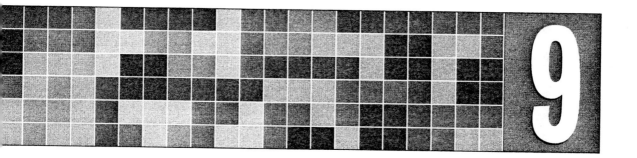

Presentation Skills

OBJECTIVE

- To apply techniques of skillful presentation to your own talks

TASKS

- Demonstrate effective use of the physical attributes of eye contact, body movement, gestures, and facial expression.
- Demonstrate effective use of the vocal qualities of quality, intelligibility, and variety.
- Discuss the importance of the five attributes of credibility.

Once the talk is prepared—organized, supported, the parts tied together with transitions, and the final presentation outline completed—success depends on the presentation skills of the speaker. Not only will an audience listen more effectively to a speaker with good presentation or delivery skills, but communication experts tell us that over half of our meaning may be communicated through these skills. A speaker's physical presence, use of the voice, and credibility with the audience are critical to the effectiveness of the presentation.

PHYSICAL BEHAVIOR

Much meaning is carried by the physical behaviors of eye contact, bodily movement, gestures, and facial expression. You need to know how the proper use of these physical behaviors can improve your speaking skill and affect your audience.

Eye Contact

Eye contact is one of the most important factors of nonverbal communication. Nothing will enhance your delivery more than effective eye contact with your audience. Eye contact is important for three reasons. First, it lets the listeners know that you are interested in them. Most people like others to look at them when talking. Second, effective eye contact allows you to receive nonverbal feedback from your audience. With good eye contact, you can gauge the effect of your remarks. You can determine if you are being understood as well as which points are making an impact and which are not. You will be able to detect signs of poor understanding and signs that the listeners are losing interest. Then you can adjust your rate of delivery or emphasis. You can rephrase or summarize certain points or add more supporting data. Third, effective eye contact enhances your credibility. Listeners judge speakers who use the greatest eye contact as being more competent than those who make little eye contact with them.

INSIGHT	*"Eyes are the windows to the soul."*
	—unknown

To achieve genuine eye contact, you must do more than merely look in the direction of your listeners. You must have an earnest desire to communicate with them. The old advice of looking over the tops of your listeners' heads or attempting to look at all parts of the audience systematically simply does not describe effective eye contact. Furthermore, looking at only one part of the audience or directing attention only to those listeners who seem to give you reinforcing feedback may cause you to ignore large parts of the audience. Show each person in a small group and each part of the audience in larger auditoriums that you are interested in them as individuals and are eager to have them understand the ideas you are presenting. In this way, you will establish mental as well as sensory contact with your listeners.

Exercise   Eye Contact

Raising hands.   Stand in front of an audience, and begin to speak. Ask all audience members to raise their hands. Tell them each one may lower his hand in turn as he feels you have established direct eye contact with him for at least three seconds. After all hands are lowered, ask each listener to reverse the process and raise his hand in turn when he feels you have established eye contact with him for at least three seconds. The objective is to get all the hands down and back up again as soon as reasonably possible.

Pass the object.   While you are speaking, ask audience members to pass a small but visible object among them. You must focus on the object. This exercise reinforces the idea that you as a speaker must pay attention to content and eye contact simultaneously.

Effective eye contact can be described as *direct* and *impartial*. You look directly into the eyes of your listeners, and you look impartially at all parts of the audience, not just at a chosen few. There are some exceptions to the rule of impartiality. For example, suppose you are making a sales presentation to a boss and her staff. In this case, you might direct more attention to the boss—the decision maker—than to her staff. Still, remember that she will most likely consult with her staff before making the decision. This situation points to the importance of knowing your audience. Who are her primary advisors? It would be wise to make frequent eye contact with them as well as with the boss. Take a tip from experienced briefers. They give primary contact to the person with the highest position—the decision maker—but they also establish effective eye contact with others in the room who will influence decisions. Remember that eye contact makes listeners feel important and included. Everyone likes to feel that way.

Body Movement

Body movement is one of the important factors of dynamic and meaningful physical behavior. Movement is important because it catches the eye of the listener. It helps to hold the attention needed for good communication. Movement can also represent a marked departure or change in your delivery pattern or a convenient way of punctuating and paragraphing your message. Listeners will know that you are finished with one idea or line of thought and ready to transition to the next. Finally, aside from its effects on the listeners, movement helps you as a presenter. It helps you work off excess energy that can promote nervousness. Movement puts you at ease.

How much movement is desirable? Some speakers seldom move yet are quite effective. However, unless the formality of the situation or the need to use a fixed microphone keeps you in one position, you may find that movement helps you communicate more effectively. Movement from behind the lectern can reduce the psychological distance between you and your listeners and put them more at ease. Some speakers feel that since they need the lectern to hold their notes, they should stay behind it. But others find it more effective to hold a note card in one hand and carry it with them, rather than looking down at the lectern to see it. But whenever you look at your notes, remember to *drop your eyes, not your head.* In other words, have your notes high enough that you can see them.

What to Call the Thing You Stand Behind

What's the thing called that you stand behind and put your notes on when you speak—a lectern, rostrum, podium, dais, pulpit, stand? A lectern or stand is the most appropriate terminology, or a pulpit if you are in a church or synagogue. A rostrum is a raised platform or stage on which a speaker stands. A lectern might be placed on a rostrum. Although the words *podium* and *dais* are sometimes mistakenly used by people when referring to a lectern, they more properly suggest a raised platform for speaking.

Of course, some speakers move too much. Perhaps out of nervousness, they pace back and forth in front of the audience. Still others have awkward movement that does not aid communication. Some leave their notes on the lectern and then move in and out from behind it like a hula dancer. Others plant their feet firmly in one place and then rock from one side to the other in regular cadence. Others try to stand beside the lectern or speaker stand but look sideways at their notes.

Effective body movement can be described as *free* and *purposeful.* You should be free to move around in front of the listeners. In most cases, you should not feel restrained to stay behind the lectern but should move with reason and purpose. Use your movement to punctuate, direct attention, and otherwise aid communication. Obviously, after-dinner speeches, briefings in a formal briefing room, and some other types of presentations don't allow for movement, and in fact, movement from behind the lectern may be inappropriate or distracting. As always, effective speakers adjust to the audience and the situation.

INSIGHT

"Every little movement has a meaning of its own."

—Otto Harbach, song lyricist

Gestures

Gestures may be used to clarify or emphasize ideas. By *gestures*, we mean the purposeful use of the hands, arms, shoulders, and head to reinforce what is being said. Fidgeting with a paper clip, rearranging and shuffling papers, and scratching your ear are not gestures. They are not purposeful, and they distract from the verbal message. Placing both hands in your pockets or behind your back or in front of you in a fig leaf position severely limits their use for gesturing. Holding your shoulders and head in one position during the talk will also rob you of an effective means of strengthening your communication.

Gestures have several functions. They can

- *emphasize.* Pointing a finger, pounding the lectern, or shaking a clenched fist each adds emphasis to what you are saying.
- *reinforce.* Holding up three fingers while saying, "I have three points to make today" reinforces your verbal message.
- *regulate.* Using gestures during a question-and-answer period can indicate when you want to talk or when you want to invite someone else to talk.
- *substitute.* Placing a finger to your puckered lips communicates "Be quiet" without your saying a word.

Here are some guidelines to help you as you work on gestures when you speak.

1. *Be relaxed.* First, although gestures can be perfected through practice, they will be most effective if you make a conscious effort to relax your muscles before you speak, perhaps by taking a few short steps or inobtrusively arranging your notes.
2. *Be natural.* While you might watch effective speakers and emulate their gestures, in most cases you will be better off doing what comes naturally to you. The same gestures you use in informal conversation are often the ones that will work best when you are speaking in front of a group.
3. *Be vigorous.* Effective gestures are complete and vigorous. Many speakers begin to gesture, but perhaps out of fear, they don't carry through and their gestures abort. This can be distracting for the audience and can even make the speaker appear ludicrous.
4. *Use good timing.* A gesture that comes after the word or phrase is spoken appears ludicrous. *Good gestures should come exactly at the time or slightly before the point is made verbally.* Poor timing often results from attempting to "can" or preplan gestures.
5. *Be versatile.* A stereotyped gesture will not fit all subjects and situations. Furthermore, the larger the audience, the more pronounced your gestures will need to be.

6. *Don't overdo them.*   Gestures should cause the audience to focus on what you are saying, not call attention to the gestures. You want the audience to remember what you say, not what you do.

7. *Make them appropriate.*   Gestures should be appropriate to the audience and the situation. Large audiences and formal speaking situations may call for bolder and more pronounced gestures. Smaller groups and less formal settings call for less formal and less pronounced gestures.

In summary, gestures should spring from within. Effective gestures are both *natural* and *spontaneous.* Observe persons talking with one another in a small group. You should try to approximate their same naturalness and spontaneity of gestures when you are speaking. The gestures you use when you are not thinking about them are most likely the ones that work best for you.

INSIGHT   *"I amused myself with trying to guess at their subject by their gestures."*

—Henry David Thoreau

Exercise   **Gestures and Movement**

Silent communication.   Communicate the following ideas silently by means of physical actions alone.

- "Get out of here!"
- "Why Tom! I haven't seen you in ages!"
- "I'd like to get to know you better."
- "Come on! Give her a chance to explain."
- "Every penny I had is gone."

Charades.   Communicate an entire message nonverbally. No spoken or written cues are permitted. For example, ask someone to demonstrate how to model a dress, do the high jump, tap dance, fly an airplane, perform the basic strokes in tennis, do a new dance step, and so forth.

Lying down.   Lie on the floor or on a table with the small of your back flat against the table. Bend your knees, with your feet remaining on the table, and stretch your arms over your head, letting the elbows and hands touch the table lightly. Your spine should be straight from top to bottom, abdomen tucked in, rib cage up, and shoulders relaxed. Get the feel of it, and then try to practice it while sitting or standing.

> *"Facial expressions and body gestures are a living language which we all have learned to read as a clue to, and use as a revelation of, character."*
>
> —Paul Zucker, author

Facial Expression

The audience looks at your face. Do you look serious when the subject is light? Do you frown when making a point? Does your facial expression match the content? You choose verbal and visual supporting material to help you make a point. Eye contact, movement, and gestures are nonverbal aids to communication, so your facial expression also should fit the content and the feeling you want to convey.

Smile. Audiences warm up to speakers who smile. Here's why. Smiles break down barriers, reduce the perceived distance between you and your listeners, cause listeners to have more confidence in what you are saying, and make you feel better and more confident in yourself. A smile creates a feeling in listeners that you are a warm human being. A smile communicates that while you believe what you are saying, you don't take yourself too seriously. We like speakers better—even intense, driven, Type A speakers—who smile. And over time, even listeners who are the "no-nonsense, down-to-business, don't waste my time with trivialities" type of individuals react better to people who smile.

Don't underestimate the importance of smiling—not a silly grin, a nervous laugh, or a perpetual "happy face," but a ready smile that communicates, "I'm real, I'm human, and I know what I'm talking about. I am a person to be listened to and trusted. I care about you."

> *"Eloquence resides as much in the tone of voice, in the eyes, and in the expression of the face, as in the choice of words."*
>
> —François, Duc De La Rochefoucauld

USE OF VOICE

A good voice has three important characteristics. It's reasonably pleasant, it's easily understood, and it expresses differences in meaning. Technically, we might label these three properties as *quality*, *intelligibility*, and *variety*. Since most people do not use their voices nearly as effectively as they could when presenting talks, this section offers several exercises to help you develop your voice.

Quality

Quality refers to the overall impression a voice makes on others. Certainly, a pleasing quality or tone is a basic component of a good speaking voice. However, vocal quality is difficult to change, and in most cases is not worth the effort. But take heart. Some of the most outstanding speakers in America have rather ordinary voices.

Dr. John Ed Mathison, senior minister of the 8,000-member Frazer United Methodist Church in Montgomery, Alabama, is one of the top preachers in America. Millions hear him each week on television. Dr. Mathison has an ordinary quality to his voice, but he demonstrates effective eye contact, movement, gestures, and facial expression. His voice demonstrates the characteristics of intelligibility and variety discussed in the next few sections. He also possesses the attributes of credibility covered later in this chapter. These characteristics and attributes, along with his excellently organized and supported sermons, make him a very compelling and engaging speaker.

You may not have a wonderfully melodious and resonant voice, but don't despair. Few people do. *It's what you do with what you've got that counts.* It may be nearly impossible to change quality, but you can use what you have to your advantage. Realize that your voice may become more breathy when you are excited, tense when suspense is involved, and resonant when reading solemn language. Listeners can often tell from the voice if the speaker is happy, angry, sad, fearful, or confident. Similarly, vocal quality can convey sincerity and enthusiasm and enhance speaker credibility in the eyes of the listeners. Don't be overly concerned about the basic quality of your voice. Do pay attention to your attitude and emotion, however. How you feel about your audience and what you are saying is more important and telling than vocal quality.

Intelligibility

Intelligibility, or the understandability of your speech, depends on several factors including articulation, pronunciation, use of pauses and expressions, and grammar.

Articulation. Articulation refers to the precision and clarity with which sounds of speech are uttered. A synonym of articulation is enunciation. Good articulation is chiefly the job of the lips, tongue, and jaw. Most articulation problems result from laziness of the tongue and lips or failure to open the mouth wide enough. You should *overarticulate* rather than *underarticulate* your speech sounds. What sounds like overarticulation to you will come out as crisp, understandable words and phrases to your listeners.

Exercise   Stretch Your Articulating Muscles

Articulation, or enunciation, is the job of the lips, tongue, and jaw. Let's stretch the muscles of articulation.

For the lips:

- Stretch your mouth in as wide a grin as possible.

- Open your mouth as wide as possible.

- Pucker your lips and protrude them as far as possible.

For the tongue:

- Stretch out your tongue as far as possible.

- Try to touch the tip of your nose and your chin with your tongue.

- Beginning at the front teeth, run the tip of your tongue back, touching the palate as far back as the tongue will go.

For the jaw:

- Lower your jaw as far as possible. Looking straight ahead, try to touch your chest with your jaw.

- Tense the muscles of the jaw. Hold that way for 5 seconds, and then relax for 10 seconds. Repeat.

Pronunciation.   This term refers to the traditional or customary utterance of words. Standards of pronunciation differ, making it difficult at times to know what is acceptable. Dictionaries are useful, but they become outdated, so don't adhere to them excessively. Generally, educated people in your community as well as national radio and television announcers provide a good standard for pronunciation. I highly recommend that you use a dictionary on-line such as *Merriam-Webster* (www.m-w.com), which allows you to click and hear the word pronounced. Common faults of pronunciation are to misplace the accent (saying *de*-vice instead of de-*vice*), to omit sounds (guh/mnt for government), to add sounds (ath*a*lete for athlete), and to sound silent letters (mor*t*gage or of*t*en).

This next point is important. Pronunciation that some consider acceptable in informal conversation may be substandard when speaking in front of a group. Never fall into the defensive mode of saying, "I grew up pronouncing words this way, and I'm not going to change now." Don't expect to adopt that attitude and still reach your potential as a speaker.

As a youngster I said "git" instead of get and "warsh" instead of wash. A college professor pointed out these and other words I mispronounced. At first I resisted. But he said, "John, you'll be a better speaker, be more successful, and sound more educated if you pronounce words correctly." I knew he was right. Even now I ask close associates and family members to listen when I speak and call pronunciation errors to my attention. I hope you do too.

Exercise   Pronouncing All the Sounds

Although the alphabet has only 26 letters, over 40 different sounds make up our words. To learn more about this, check out the International Phonetic Association website at www.arts.gla.ac.uk/IPA. Unless you are highly unusual, you will have little interest in understanding the differences among plosive, fricative, nasal, vowel, and diphthong sounds, but you do need to say the sounds correctly. So here is a list that covers the 41 basic sounds minus the phonetic designation. Say these words to your teacher, trainer, or someone who hears and pronounces words well. All the basic sounds of the language are captured several times.

- Paul looked up at the ripest plum on the tree.
- Bob was barely able to carry the books.
- Tell the teacher the boys are fighting.
- Don't send the letter to the old address.
- The class brought a sack of candy to the circus.
- The big man is lagging behind the smaller one.
- Some of the ball bats are missing.
- The zeal of the players was amazing.
- Frank was laughing at the giraffe.
- Vera and the other wives are leaving.
- She put ashes instead of sugar in the mash.
- He had a vision of a new garage painted azure.
- Both of the thin men were affected by ether.
- Either breathe in this way or give up swimming.
- Henry heard that it was bad to inhale.
- The man attempted to move his right arm.

- No one knew what happened in the ninth inning.

- Ring out the old, the chorus sang.

- Leo heard the bell tolling in the loft.

- The writer drove over the road himself.

- Will fixes the wagons in the winter.

- The white foxes howl when he whistles.

- Yesterday you argued for the union.

- We feel that the reed needs adjusting.

- He did not intend to hit the little boy.

- In September Ned received a pen and pencil set.

- He received a bad gash in the back.

- Father arrived on a calm day in October.

- He saw a lawyer before he bought the loft.

- He took as good a look as he could.

- Two pairs of boots were found under the stool.

- He loved his sons very much.

- Among the items was the editor's sofa.

- Myrtle firmly believed the fur was mink.

- He is a better sailor than any of the others.

- Make a new date two weeks later.

- The old man told a long, sad story.

- A few more feuds will give the law a cue.

- I said fix the tire, not the fire.

- No houses are built in the downtown district.

- After much toil the men brought in the oil well.

Practice saying words and sounds correctly that you have trouble with. The ancient Grecian orator Demosthenes is reputed to have overcome articulation and pronunciation problems by going to the seashore and placing a handful of pebbles in his mouth while speaking toward the sea. But you can do the same thing by exercising your face, jaw, and mouth muscles.

| INSIGHT | According to Plutarch, "Demosthenes overcame and rendered more distinct his inarticulate and stammering pronunciation by speaking with pebbles in his mouth." But don't try this technique! First, rocks may be dirty. Second, swallowing pebbles would not be good. |

Exercise   Practicing Some Tongue Twisters

You can compile your own list of tongue twisters. There are many web sites that specialize in them. Here are a few short examples for a start.

- A big black bug bit a big black bear. But where is the big black bear that the big black bug bit?
- A big bug bit the little beetle, but the little beetle bit the big bug back.
- A box of mixed biscuits in a mixed biscuit box.
- An ape hates grape cakes.
- A skunk sat on a stump. The stump thought the skunk stunk. The skunk thought the stump stunk. Which stunk more—the skunk or the stump?
- Baboon, bamboo, baboon, bamboo, baboon, bamboo, baboon, bamboo.
- He sawed six long, slim, sleek, slender saplings.
- Rubber baby buggy bumpers.

Vocalized pauses. This is the name we give to syllables "a," "uh," "um," and "ah," which are often used at the beginning of a sentence. While a few vocalized pauses are natural and do not distract, too many impede the communication process.

Overuse of stock expressions. Stock phrases, such as "OK," "like," and "you know," should be avoided. These expressions serve no positive communicative function and only convey a lack of originality by the speaker.

Exercise   Getting Rid of Troublesome Words

Place troublesome words or phrases, such as "OK," "er," "uhm," "and a," and "you know," on 3 × 5 cards so the speaker can see them as she speaks. A variation is for each audience member to have a card with the troublesome word or phrase on it. When the speaker uses the word or phrase, audience members hold up their cards. Be careful using this variation, however, for it can be extremely distracting to the speaker.

Use of substandard grammar. Substandard grammar has no place in speaking. It will serve only to reduce your credibility with some listeners. Research shows that even persons who have been using substandard grammar all of their lives can, with diligent practice, make significant gains in this area in a relatively short time.

Variety

Variety is the spice of speaking. Listeners tire rapidly when listening to a speaker who doesn't vary her delivery style or a speaker who has a monotonous voice. A speaker's voice that is intelligible and has good quality still may not appeal to listeners. You may vary your voice and at the same time improve the communication by considering the vocal fundamentals of rate, volume, force, pitch, and emphasis.

Rate. Most people speak at a rate of from 100 to 160 words a minute when presenting a talk. In normal speech, however, we vary the rate often so that even within the 100- to 160-word constraints there is much change. The temperamentally excitable person may speak at a rapid rate all the time, and the stolid person generally talks in a slow drawl. The enthusiastic but confident individual, however, will vary the rate of delivery to emphasize ideas and feelings. A slower rate may be appropriate for presenting main points, while a more rapid rate may lend itself to support material. The experienced speaker also knows that an occasional pause punctuates thought and emphasizes ideas. A dramatic pause at the proper time may express feelings and ideas even more effectively than words.

She talked at 100 miles an hour, with gusts up to 150.	**INSIGHT**

Exercise   Adjusting Your Rate

Read the following sentences at an appropriate rate—slow, fast, or medium. Then try reading them at an inappropriate rate.

- The day is cold and dark and dreary.

- I just love it when that happens.

- There's nothing like a nice walk in the park to make you feel really good.

- It was the most exciting race I ever saw.

- How about coming over to my place tonight?

- I want you to stop beating up your brother right now; do you hear me?

Volume. Volume is important to the speaker. Always be certain that the entire audience can hear you. Nothing hinders the effect of a talk more than to have some listeners unable to hear. On the other hand, the talk should not be too loud for a small room. A bombastic or overly loud speaker tires listeners out very quickly.

Exercise   Changing Your Volume

Read the following sentences three ways: first, as though your listener were 3 feet away; second, as though he were 10 feet away; and third, as though he were 100 feet away.

- Come here, Martha.
- Throw the ball to me.
- Bring me two bottles.
- What did you say?
- Tell that to your mother.

Read each of the following sayings twice—first, quite loud, and then softly.

- Act in haste; repent at leisure.
- A rolling stone gathers no moss.
- A stitch in time saves nine.
- Look before you leap; he who hesitates is lost.

Force. Force is needed at times to emphasize and dramatize ideas. A drowsy audience will come to attention quickly if the speaker uses force effectively. At times, a sudden reduction in force may be as effective as a rapid increase. By learning to control the force of your voice, you can help to add emphasis and improve communication.

Exercise   Controlling Your Force

Vary the force for each of these statements according to the instructions.

1. "I hate you! I hate you! I hate you! I hate you! I hate you!"
   - Increase the degree of force each time until the last time is almost a shout.
   - Shout the first time, and then get progressively softer until you almost whisper the last one.

2. "If I've told you once, I've told you a hundred times."

- Make the statement as a straightforward assertion, using a sustained force.
- Speak the sentence with a sudden explosion of force, expressing anger.
- Speak the sentence with deep but controlled emotion and firm, steady force.

3. "Ah, sweet mystery of love."

- Repeat the statement several times emphasizing a different word each time. Don't vary pitch, just force.
- Repeat the statement first as a sentiment, then as an explanation, and finally as a question.

Pitch.   Pitch is the highness or lowness of the voice. All things being equal, a higher-pitched voice carries better than a low-pitched one. On the other hand, listeners will tend to tire faster when listening to the higher-pitched voice. If your voice is within normal limits—neither too high nor too low— work for variety as you speak.

Exercise   Varying Your Pitch

Follow the directions for each of these exercises, attempting to vary only your pitch.

- Read the following sentence aloud, stressing a different word each time you read it; notice that seven different meanings are achieved simply by changing the pitch of a word: "Martha Smith told me about the test."
- Say the following words:
    Who, what, when, why, where, how
  using five different inflection patterns: (1) level, (2) rising, (3) falling, (4) rising/falling, (5) falling/rising.
- Vary the pitch to change the meaning as you say the following statement: "Yes, I really did enjoy going to the game with Bill, except for the fact that it rained the whole time and my team lost. Don't rub it in. You know I get angry when you make fun of me that way. How would you feel if I said things to hurt you?"

Emphasis.   Emphasis obviously stems from all forms of vocal variety, and any change in rate, force, or pitch will influence the emphasis. The greater or more sudden the change, the greater the emphasis will be. As a speaker, you must use emphasis wisely. Two things should be avoided: *overemphasis* and *continual* emphasis. Be judicious. Emphasizing a point beyond its real value may cause you to lose credibility with your listeners.

Exercise   Influencing the Emphasis

To develop vocal variety, read the following statements at least five different ways, each time changing the rate, volume, pitch, and force. Be sure to maintain the full meaning of each statement, making it as interesting and as engaging as possible.

- An old clock, which had stood in the family kitchen for 50 years or more without giving its owner any cause for complaint, early one Sunday morning, before any of the family were stirring, suddenly stopped.

- We started for the woods early one Saturday morning when all of a sudden something black appeared near the path. Alice grabbed my arm and started to scream. She thought it was a bear, but it was only a big black stump.

- Oh, I don't know. I have heard people say that before, but I am sure it will be a long, long time before we live in a world of permanent peace.

INSIGHT   *"In speech, we safeguard meaning by the use of intonation, stress, gesture, and voice qualities."*

—Harold Whitehall, author

CREDIBILITY

All the factors discussed thus far influence the audience's perception of speaker credibility. Adequate and appropriate preparation of the material, effective organization, the use of engaging verbal and visual supporting material, the right kind of humor, and a good beginning and ending will all enhance your credibility as a speaker. In fact, these factors are key to establishing credibility with your listeners. But once your talk is prepared and well in hand, the single biggest factor is delivery—how the talk is presented. In addition to the earlier discussions about method of delivery, control of nervousness, physical behavior, and use of voice, five attributes of delivery are important: competence, trustworthiness, enthusiasm, adaptability, and sincerity.

INSIGHT   *Speakers' credibility rests in the minds of their listeners.*

Competence

In Chapter 4, we said that the effectiveness of statistics and testimony depends on whether they come from expert or competent sources. So too, your audience must perceive you as either competent or expert. A physician speaking on the necessity of an annual checkup, a mechanic discussing the importance of rotating tires on your automobile, and a tax accountant speaking on new changes in filing your income tax would be examples of people who possess expertise on their subjects. They are competent sources.

Often, the audience knows that speakers are competent before they begin. One reason speakers are often introduced by someone else is to establish the speaker's competence or expertise on the subject. This is referred to as *initial* competence; it's what the audience judges the speaker's competence to be before the presentation begins. On the other hand, *internal* competence is what speakers reveal as they talk.

If an audience knows my reputation and an introducer builds me up to the audience, then I have initial competence. If I do a credible job while speaking and demonstrate I know my subject, I provide internal evidence of my competence. Also, if while speaking on the subject "How to Speak Effectively," I mention that I received my Ph. D. in speech communication over 30 years ago or that I give several speeches or presentations each week, these facts help to internally establish my credibility on the subject. These facts would not make me a credible speaker on the subject "How to Operate Heavy Equipment." The facts must fit the subject.

You must be careful when attempting to enhance your own credibility. It may backfire. If you come across as boasting or bragging, you will turn off many in the audience. I might state the preceding facts about me this way: "Over 30 years ago, when I was working on my Ph. D. degree in communication, I wondered if I would ever finish. But I finally did." Or I might say, "Even though I give several speeches or presentations each week, I still have a lot to learn about speaking." These statements convey the same information in a more self-deprecating way.

The audience must perceive the speaker as competent. If not, they most likely won't listen. And even if they do listen, they may discount much of what the speaker says.

"Yeah, I think the speaker is an expert on something, but not on what he was talking about."

INSIGHT

—overheard after a speech

Trustworthiness

As with competence, initial trustworthiness is what speakers bring to the speech. A well-known public servant, an old friend, and a person who has a reputation of helping others rather than behaving in a self-serving way are examples of speakers with outstanding *initial* trustworthiness. Good introductions by someone the audience respects can help establish initial trust in the speaker. But speakers must build and maintain trust as they speak. *Internal* trustworthiness cannot be established by simply saying, "Trust me." Trust is earned by speaking intelligently, openly, and without bias. Salespeople have a difficult time building internal credibility since if they make a sale, it means money in their pockets. You build trust easiest when you have nothing to gain. This is why outside negotiators often mediate a dispute. Senior statespersons are asked to provide advice and counsel to those active in corporate or political arenas because they have no "dog in the fight," or stake in the outcome.

You build trustworthiness by communicating a genuine interest in your audience. This goes back to an early lesson in this book: an effective presentation is listener centered. An audience will be motivated to listen to you and believe you only if they trust you.

Enthusiasm

Whereas competence and trustworthiness can be initial—that is, established before the speakers ever utter a word—this is not so for enthusiasm. Enthusiasm, excitement, positive energy, dynamism—these all spring from the speaker's delivery of the presentation and involvement with the material and the audience. Interesting examples, humorous illustrations, a dynamic physical presence, and a commanding voice all provide positive energy and enthusiasm to the presentation. Charisma is a form of energy and dynamism. Some people project charm, magnetism, and an attractiveness that make people want to listen. It all starts with attitude.

INSIGHT   *Enthusiasm is contagious, and so is the lack of it.*

Think about days when you've felt really good about yourself and life. Contrast such days to ones when you felt "down" or felt that things weren't going well for you. Guess which days you projected the most positive energy and enthusiasm. Experienced speakers know that to do the best job speaking, they must possess positive enthusiasm. That's why in Chapter 8 when I suggested getting rid of nervous energy, I cautioned against using alcohol or drugs, which can take your energy. Positive energy and enthusiasm come from a positive attitude. Hang around encouragers rather than discouragers when you are about to make a presentation.

Adaptability

Adjust to your audience. Don't let little things bother you, such as an out-of-sync slide, a mispronounced word, or a minor interruption. Handling unexpected problems draws your audience closer to you and inspires their confidence in you. Here are some examples of adaptability.

■ *You keep calm after you forget what comes next.*   Don't panic—simply go back and summarize what you have said so far. Usually, you will remember what follows. If you don't, say, "Just a minute. I got lost." Take a few seconds, find your place, and then continue.

■ *You know what is appropriate dress for the occasion.*   It's always better to overdress than underdress. However, I unintentionally carried this to an extreme once. Some years ago, I got mixed up on the type of occasion and showed up for a speech in a neighboring state dressed in a tuxedo, but no one else even had a tie. That occasion was "casual night"; the next night was formal. I didn't let it bother me. I took a few good-natured jabs in stride, made a joke of it by saying "This is the way we always dress in Alabama when we go to a barbeque," took off my coat and tie, and gave my speech. By the way, this faux pas would not be nearly as serious as showing up casual when the audience is in formal attire.

■ *When someone asks you a question for which you don't know the answer, don't step away.*   Instead, confidently and slowly take a step toward them. This gives you time to think and communicates that you are pleased they asked the question. Then either answer it or, if you can't, just say, "Good question. I don't have a good answer, but I'll find out and get back to you." Then make certain you do. Don't say, "I'm glad you asked that question," when you really wish they had not asked it. It comes across as phony because it is.

■ *When a cell phone rings, you don't act perturbed, make a wisecrack, or embarrass the person.*   He probably feels bad enough already. If he doesn't, your comment won't register with him anyway. And besides, others in the audience will think less of you if you comment. Just continue as if it doesn't bother you. You will win points from your audience.

■ *The projector quits and you can't show your PowerPoint slides, but (as advised in Chapter 6) you have a contingency plan.*   If you are at a good spot for a break, stop and regroup. If not, press on.

The bottom line is to be listener centered—not message centered or self-centered. Being listener centered implies adaptability. And your adaptability as a presenter to your audience will go a long way toward establishing your credibility.

INSIGHT	*"You can't step into the same stream twice."*
	—Heraclitus

Sincerity

Ironically, one of the most important attributes (and, for that matter, one of the most important points in this book) can be covered with just a few words. You certainly need to prepare well and possess strong delivery skills to do an effective job in front of a group. You must come across as competent (knowing what you are talking about), trustworthy (worthy of belief), enthusiastic (caring about your subject), and adjustable (adapting to your listeners and the occasion as you speak). But something more is needed. To be really effective, you must be sincere. As long as you obviously try to generate light and not merely heat (in other words, to enlighten your listeners and not just go through the routine of giving a talk), listeners will be amazingly tolerant of weaknesses in both preparation and delivery. But give them a chance to suspect your sincerity, and you lose effectiveness. Once lost, effectiveness is nearly impossible to regain. What is sincerity? It is a demonstration that you are without deceit, pretense, or hypocrisy. You are perceived as being honest, truthful, and faithful.

You must communicate authenticity about three things. Sincerity toward your *listeners* is reflected in your eye contact, enthusiasm, and concern about the audience members as individuals. Sincerity toward your *subject* is judged by whether or not you seem involved and interested in what you are talking about. Sincerity toward *self* is displayed in the confidence and concern you have that you are doing the best job possible.

FOLLOW THE GOLDEN RULE

Do unto others as you would have them do unto you. The central focus of all communication is other-directedness or listener-centeredness. There are exceptions to almost everything I have said in this book. There are times when you can make a statement and will need no supporting material. There are times when a speech does not need a good beginning or ending. There are times when clear organization is not important. All these "rules" have exceptions; the Golden Rule does not. The effective presenter is always other directed, focused on the audience. Be the kind of presenter you want others to be when you are in the audience. Ask yourself, "How would I want someone to speak to me?" That's how you should speak to others.

"Therefore, however you want people to treat you, so treat them, for this is the Law and the Prophets."

INSIGHT

—Jesus, as recorded in Matthew 7:12 NASB

Check Yourself: What Have You Learned?

- ☐ Effective physical behavior is characterized by direct and impartial eye contact, free and purposeful movement, natural and spontaneous gestures, and appropriate facial expression.
- ☐ Quality, intelligibility, and variety are key characteristics of vocal behavior.
- ☐ Speaker credibility depends on competence, trustworthiness, enthusiasm, adaptability, and sincerity.
- ☐ Practice and use of exercises will help you improve your skills
- ☐ Treat your audience the way you want to be treated—be listener centered.

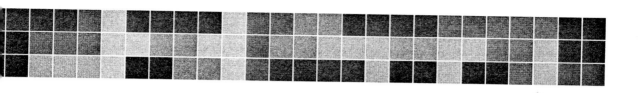

Index